STOCK OPTIONS: THE GREATEST WEALTH BUILDING TOOL EVER INVENTED

Daniel Mollat

For information regarding special discounts for bulk purchases, please contact BN Publishing at
info@bnpublishing.net

www.bnpublishing.net

Printed in the U.S.A.

TABLE OF CONTENTS

FOREWORD

In this book winning option trader Daniel Mollat shares an option trading system with a high probability of success. He shows readers how to change from being the gambler to the casino operator with the system that he has used for excellent returns with limited risk for over a decade.

This is exactly the kind of trading book I like to read. A real trader discussing how he makes money in the market, with real trades. This is what you want to see, not theories and back testing, but real life winning at trading. Mr. Mollat gives traders what they need to be successful, a trading method, risk management, and real trade examples. He respects the unpredictability of the market and trades re-actively to what is actually going on, no predicting required, just trading the market action and the odds.

I agree with his proven system. Selling out of the money calls and puts short is the best way I have also found to put the odds of success in your favor. He discusses in great detail how to use one of my personal favorite option strategies: the short strangle. In the strategy explained in this book you will see how to sell both a call and a put on a stock or ETF to double your chances of success. He follows up these recommendations with how to manage the risk of these positions through using ratio credit spreads, but not until they are needed. He gives the great advice to use index ETF options as the underlying stock to limit risk and only trade the most highly liquid ETFs.

This book is a solid addition to any library of option trading books. It can show you how to put the odds of winning at options squarely in your favor.

Steve Burns

Author of: New Trader, Rich Trader and How I Made Money Using the Nicolas Darvas System

PREFACE

Options, whether they be derivatives of stocks, commodities, futures, or other financial instruments, are complex in nature and must be understood fully in order for one to make the most out of them. Having said this, don't be frightened by the word complex. It is by reading books like this that you will learn to demystify the complexity of options. In your learning process do not feel overwhelmed by all the mumbo jumbo about this lucrative investment instrument even if you believe that you are just an ordinary person in the street. I am just an ordinary man in the street like yourself who learned to trade options by teaching myself. In the early days when options were some kind of novelty, only financial professionals used them in the marketplace. There were very few books and teaching materials on the subject. You can then appreciate what I've gone through in my learning process. Most of what I know today has been learned in the school of hard knocks, by actually diving in the market and learning from my own mistakes and successes. Today, with options becoming phenomenally popular with the investing public there are now quite a number of books, web sites, blogs, investment forums, and schools that are dedicated to teaching options. Still, the complexities of various option trading strategies continue to overwhelm investors and it is my hope that this book will present a simple teaching method of what may be to some a complex trading system.

I have been involved with the stock market and its derivatives for nearly forty years. When I started dabbling in the stock market my main objective was to find an investment system or trading strategy that would give me decent returns and yet be a safe investment for the long haul. I must admit that over the years I've encountered many disappointments and, on occasions, incurred losses as I stumbled and recovered in my learning process. My objective of finding the Holy Grail of investments eluded me constantly but I can say that in the process of my long search I gained a wealth of knowledge about the securities industry and its derivatives.

For a long time I tried investments in the stock market and while I was fairly successful in this, with winnings slightly ahead of losses, the end result over a period of time was no better than if I had just left my money in the money market or invested in treasury bills. I even tried commodity futures trading for a while and quickly discovered that this arena is strictly for professionals who are deeply immersed in the world of commodities. Amateurs like me had no business being in commodity futures. Then I got into stock mutual funds. For a while these were much better than direct investments in individual stocks and I was pleased with the returns. But during downturns in the economy and the stock market, mutual funds could take as bad a beating as the market. So on with my search for the Holy Grail of investments.

It was in the late eighties when I discovered stock options. The wealth building properties of stock options truly fascinated me and for the next several years I got very involved with options trading. During the hot market of the nineties my options trading activities rode the crest of success until the stock market collapse of 2001-2002. The trading strategies that I successfully employed during the hot market days just didn't work anymore and I suffered heavy losses during this recessionary period. I was trading mostly long positions, that is, buying calls and puts. It never occurred to me to look at the other side of options trading and that is, being the seller instead of the buyer of options. During the recessionary years following the 2001-2002 economic downturn I began seriously looking at the strategy of selling options.

This book, while giving the novice trader a basic education in options and what this phenomenon is all about, will mainly talk about a very special area of options trading. I will be discussing in great detail how the strategy of selling options can be an excellent tool for the long term investor who is in search of an investment vehicle that will provide him with steady, above average returns year in year out. The option selling program outlined in this book is the result of my own trading experience in selling options over the past ten years. I have back tested the system and used the trading technique in the year 2001 when the stock market declined by nearly 50% and, I'm pleased to say it did quite well under the conditions then prevailing. An investment in the system made prior to the collapse would have held its value better than anything then available in the investment world. You will see what I mean when you come to the part in the book where I present actual trading illustrations.

I've read many books and articles on various option strategies with particular emphasis on selling options and there is one thing that I find missing in all these materials. I have not found a book that describes in great detail what an option seller should do when the market turns against him. While all materials about selling options do mention corrective measures to be taken when negative forces come into play there is not one that goes into a methodical, deep and thorough explanation of what steps the option seller should take in a reversing market. This book addresses this very important issue with much detail and gives actual trading illustrations of what to do. In short, the book offers a step by step handholding experience of how to avoid taking a loss in the event that the market moves against the option seller. Nearly half of this book is dedicated to providing actual trading transactions over a period of many months.

Further, it is my intention to make selling options available to every Tom, Dick and Harry without the need for the individual to be knowledgeable in the fundamentals and technicals of the stock market. I myself, even to this day, continue my option selling activities without devoting much time and attention getting into the fundamentals and technicals of market behavior. My system is designed for the investor to trade options in reaction rather than in anticipation of the market's behavior. You will see the meaning of this as you follow the trades illustrated in this book. Every book on option trading strategies have the authors recommending trading strategies based on the assumptions about the trader's perception of market direction. What they are saying is that you should use the trading strategy that would work best with the way you anticipate the market's movement. But it's impossible to predict the market! It has been said, and I fully subscribe to this thinking, that "the stock market is a random walk down Wall Street". Even the highly paid experts in the financial world can't predict the market with consistent accuracy, so how can you and I, non-professionals, even attempt to do so? My trading system is based not on how we foresee market direction but on the assumption that we don't know where the market will go and we trade only in reaction to its movement not in anticipation of it. As I said before, I invested in mutual funds for many years and I can tell you there are very few, if any, funds that outperform the market consistently year in, year out. What does this tell you? That despite the millions of dollars at their disposal for research and studies even the most highly paid investment experts cannot predict the market's direction with infallible accuracy.

By purchasing this book I'm assuming you have some familiarity with options, what they are, what they can do and how you can use them to enhance your trading and investment programs. It is important that you have a good basic understanding of how options behave to fully grasp and understand the methods outlined in this book. The first chapters of this book deal with basic information about options which I hope would be sufficient to enable you to follow the book intelligently. Once you become proficient in the option selling strategy that is outlined here, you can go forward and explore other option selling techniques that will further enhance your trading and investment returns.

CHAPTER ONE

History and development of options

If you owned stock and wanted to buy insurance against a drop in your stock's value would there be such a thing? No, but you could have such protection by creating your own insurance program. How? Via stock options!

If you owned stock in a well established company yet you receive small dividends, or none at all, you could increase or pay yourself cash dividends in another way. How? Via stock options!

If you wanted to buy stock in a company but you would like its price to drop to a certain level before committing your purchase you could start profiting from that stock while waiting for its price to drop. How? Via stock options!

If you wish to diversify your investment in various stocks yet do not have sufficient funds to spread your money around you could still put together a diversified portfolio. How? Via stock options!

Want to sell stocks short but can't stomach the risk that goes with it? You can do it with options with very little risk involved!

Do you have funds earning meager interests in cash accounts such as CDs or savings deposits? Use options as a means of increasing returns.

The above benefits offered by stock options are but a few of the numerous ways available to stock investors in managing and controlling risk in the stock market. For this reason options markets have sprouted swiftly and continues to grow in popularity in many parts of the world.

Historically options have been around for many centuries but as it is traded today it is relatively a new phenomenon. It was in 1973 that options were born in the form that they are today. Before then options were mostly traded by farmers and commodity traders seeking price stability in their products. They were widely traded as a means of price protection for their products. It enabled these early businessmen to lock in future prices thus offering greater stability in the market. While these price protection contracts served the purpose of maintaining stability in the marketplace, they were seldom used as instruments of trade mainly because they lacked the element of liquidity. All this changed in 1973 when the Chicago Board Options Exchange (CBOE) was created and the first options exchange came into being. The CBOE began offering listed options in a standardized form making it easy and convenient for buyers and sellers to trade these instruments and creating therefore a system of matching buy and sell orders quickly and in an orderly fashion. At this point options trading was quite limited but later, in 1975, the Options Clearing Corporation was created to serve as a central clearing facility for other types of options offered to the general public. While slow to gain popularity initially options have consistently grown acceptance among investors resulting in an explosive growth rate in the 90s which is still currently going on today.

Today the popularity of options trading continues to grow exponentially and according to the Options Industry Council option contracts traded in the US in 2007 was just short of 3 billion whereas in 1999 it stood at 507 million. This is a growth rate of nearly 600% in just seven years! In 2010 there were some 4 billion option contracts traded. The volume traded in 2010 marks the eighth consecutive year a new annual trading volume record has been set. In addition to hitting new annual volume records, the following records were set in the year 2010.

- Highest single trading day in 2010 for total options (stocks, commodities, futures): May 6 with 30,818,984 contracts
- Highest single trading day ever for equity (stock) options: December 16 with 29,352,698 contracts
- Average daily total options volume: 15,472,494
- Average daily equity options volume: 14,327,131
- Options Premium: $1.2 trillion changed hands, which is about the same amount as 2009.

Among the countries that immediately recognized the benefits offered by options, Australia became the first foreign country to follow suit in 1976 when it opened its own Australian Options Market. Seeing the success of options in the US and Australian markets, Europe rapidly followed the trend with many countries coming on board this rapidly developing derivative product where it is now enjoying tremendous trading volume. In Asia, Hong Kong followed several years later subsequently overtaking Australia in trading volume and today is Asia's most active stock options market.

The birth of the options market spawned the creation of dozens of trading strategies and systems that is today being used not only by financial institutions but also by individual options traders. Stock options as an investment instrument is now widely employed as a safe and sound money management strategy. The ability of options to give the investor a wide range of choices in stock market investment is what has made the options market grow by leaps and bounds over the last two or three decades. There are dozens of option trading systems being employed by individual investors as well as financial institutions. Each system is designed to accomplish a specific investment goal. A financial institution may use long put options to hedge its winnings in stocks that have appreciated in value, another investor may buy call options instead of stocks to enter a position in a security that has caught his fancy. Still another may sell calls against his stock holdings to generate income (like dividends) from his stock position, or what is popularly known as covered call writing.

So what is causing this phenomenal growth and popularity in options trading? The answer can be found in the first five statements in this chapter. The advantages presented by options trading has not only appealed to institutional investors but to individual traders as well. In the US the bulk of all options contracts are traded by individual investors.

So what exactly are options?

Options defined

An option is a contract giving the buyer the right, but not the obligation, to buy or sell an underlying asset (stocks, commodities, futures, or indexes) at a specific price on or before a certain date. An option is not a tangible product but a right or privilege to acquire, own or dispose of a tangible asset. It is what is called a derivative financial instrument, that is, its value is derived from a tangible product that gives it this right or privilege. In the case of a stock option, its value is based on the underlying stock. In the case of an index option, its value is based on the underlying index representing a basket of securities. Since an option has value derived from its underlying asset it can be traded just like any security such as a stock or bond, and constitutes a binding contract with strictly defined terms and properties.

If you have ever had some exposure in the real estate business you will surely have come across real estate agreements that carried provisions for what is normally termed earnest money or non-refundable deposit in exchange for the right to buy, sell or rent a piece of property. By tendering earnest money or non-refundable deposit the contracting parties are entering into an agreement where one side acquires the right to either buy, sell or rent a piece of property at a fixed agreed price and the right is exercisable over a fixed period of time. After the specified period of time has elapsed the right expires and becomes null and void. This in effect is an option contract where one of the parties bought or sold an option to buy, sell or rent property. Call it real estate option if you wish

Let's look at it another way. Suppose you are a wholesaler of produce and you have customers who are extremely sensitive to changing market prices and you are asked to guarantee that your produce prices will remain stable at all times. You tell them not to worry and assure them that it will be the case. In order for you to grant such assurance you in turn must have some kind of guarantee from the farmer from whom you purchase products. You therefore talk to your farmer supplier and ask him to give you the right to purchase all of his next coming harvest at a pre agreed price no matter what market conditions prevail at the time of harvest. Assuming the farmer's estimated future harvest has a total value $10,000 in today's prices, you offer him $1,000 as good faith money or earnest money or premium money for the right to buy (option) his products or to be the first to buy his crop with the condition that if you decide to exercise your right he is obligated to sell his entire harvest at the agreed price of $10,000. If you eventually decide not to want to purchase his products you may walk away from your commitment without further obligation to him. The earnest money or premium that you paid the farmer is not refundable and the farmer gets to keep it whether you exercise your right or not. If you do decide to purchase his products you still need to pay him $10,000 which means your total cost is $11,000 when you factor in the $1,000 earnest money.

The farmer accepts your offer and takes your $1,000 good faith money. You have just entered into an options contract with the farmer giving you the right, but not the obligation, to purchase his entire crop of produce at harvest time at a predetermined price of $10,000. If at harvest time, due to seasonal conditions such as a draught, causes the farmer's products to command higher pricing, say $12,500, the farmer will have no choice but to honor his contract and sell to you at the pre agreed price of $10,000.

In the above example, you the wholesaler bought the right ($1,000) to purchase goods at a predetermined price ($10,000) for a fixed period of time (harvest time) as protection for any possible future increase in price.

Now let's put you as the farmer and look at the scenario on the farmer's side. As you are doing your preparations during the planting season you feel insecure about the future pricing structure of your products. You would be happy to get $10,000 for your goods regardless if prices turn out to be much higher at harvest time. But you certainly would not be happy if for any reason your harvested crops end up valued at much less than your desired $10,000. To protect yourself you approach a wholesaler and offer him $1,000 to acquire the right to sell to him your entire crop at a fixed, guaranteed price of $10,000. You are merely purchasing the right to sell (option) to the wholesaler but you are not obligated to sell if you choose not to. In either case, whether you elect to sell or not, you lose the $1,000 good faith money or premium you paid.

Fast forward to harvest time. If conditions are such that your harvest is now worth a mere $8,000 you can then exercise your option sell to the wholesaler at the pre agreed price of $10,000. Obviously you are still in the hole for $1,000 which is the price you paid for the option to sell. But losing $1,000 is much better than losing $2,000 if you had not bought the option to sell. On the other hand if your goods are now worth $12,000, then you can choose not to exercise your right to sell and therefore you are free to offer to others at current market prices. After deducting your $1,000 cost of the option to sell, you still end up gaining $1,000 at harvest time.

What have just been illustrated are examples of the functions of call options and put options. In the first example the wholesaler bought a call option to protect himself against a possible rise in prices while in the second example the farmer bought a put option to protect himself against a drop in prices.

As you have seen options are classed into two main groups, calls and puts.

Calls and Puts defined

In the world of financial securities the situation is very similar to the farmer and wholesaler. In the stock market a call option grants the option holder the right to buy a stock at a specified price on or before a certain date. A stock call option therefore is like the earnest money that the produce wholesaler put up. The price paid for a call option is called the option premium and the guaranteed price that you have bought protection for is called the strike price or exercise price. The option you bought carries an expiration date at which time your right granted by owning the option expires and becomes null and void. You must therefore exercise your right to buy the stock on or before the expiration date if you decide that you do want to buy the underlying stock. If you decide not to exercise your right (option) to buy the stock--and you are not obligated to do so--your only cost is the option premium.

Example: You have $10,000 cash and wish to buy Microsoft (stock symbol MSFT) but you're afraid that the stock may drop soon after you buy its shares. Your $10,000 would buy 403 shares at its current price of $24.80. Because of your uncertain view of Microsoft, you elect to purchase call options instead of committing your entire capital at this point. You feel that if the stock goes in a rising trend you would then not mind taking a position in Microsoft. But in the meantime you make a decision that instead of buying shares outright you will take an option to buy the stock within the next 90 days. You call your broker and give him the order to purchase 4 call option contracts of MSFT 25 (25 is the guaranteed price for the stock) at the current premium price of $0.52. All options contracts are quoted in multiples of 100 shares. Your total cost is therefore is 4 (contracts) x 100 (shares per contract) x $0.52 (option premium per share) = $208. You have just entered into a contract where you have acquired the right to purchase Microsoft shares at a guaranteed price of $25 and you have 90 days to decide whether to exercise your right or not. For this privilege of a $25 guaranteed price you paid a premium of $208 for 4 contracts (400 shares). Now you are in control of 400 shares of MSFT without owning the stock. If you had purchased the 400 shares as you originally planned at the current price of $24.80 your total investment would be $$9,920 instead of just $208 for the 4 call option contracts. If within the next 90 days Microsoft rises to $27.25, you can exercise your call options and buy 400 shares at the guaranteed price of $25 thereby making your net cost to own the stock at a mere $25.52 ($25 plus $0.52 option premium). Now you own 400 shares of MSFT at a cost of $25.52 when the shares are today trading at $27.25 thereby affording you an immediate paper profit of $1.73 per share.

In the real world, if your intention is to make a profit from stock and options trading it is unlikely you would want to exercise your call options. The reason being that if MSFT did rise to $27.25 the market value of your call options would likewise rise but at a more aggressive rate than the share price. With MSFT at $27.25 your call options could easily be priced at around $3.00. You could just sell your 4 call contracts at $3.00 and make a profit of $992 (4 contracts x 100 shares per contract x $3.00) instead of $1.73 per share (total $692) if you exercised your option. But if your intention is to own Microsoft shares in the hope of long term rewards, electing to exercise would be the better choice.

Let's say that instead of going up MSFT shares started retreating shortly after you purchased your call options. It continued its downward slide so that by the end of the 90 day validity period the price is quoted at $21.15. In this instance you can just walk away from your options contract and let it expire. You lose the $208 you paid for the calls but you saved yourself the potential of losing $1,460 if you had purchased the shares at its original price of $24.80. Furthermore, you are now presented with the opportunity of purchasing MSFT at the much lower price of $21.15. If you did this your cost would be $21.15 plus the $0.52 premium you originally paid for a total cost of $21.67, still much lower than if you had purchased the stock 90 days earlier at the price of $24.80.

A Put option is the opposite of a call option. Whereas a call option gives the holder the right but not the obligation to buy stock, a put option grants the holder the right but not the obligation to sell a stock at a specified price on or before a specific date. This function of a put option is similar to buying insurance against a drop in the price of the stock you hold. This is what was meant by the first statement in this chapter that options can be used like insurance against a drop in a stock price. It can therefore be said that with a put option you can buy insurance to fix the selling price of your stock for a given period of time. This is the same as buying house insurance where you buy protection for a given period of time.

Using the same scenario on Microsoft, let's assume you are the holder or owner of 500 shares of the stock which you purchased several months ago at a price of $20.36 for a total investment of $10,180. Microsoft is now trading at a price of $24.80. You are pleased at the thought that you have gained a profit by $4.44 per share on your Microsoft holdings for a total paper profit of $2,220 on your 500 shares. But at the same time you are getting jitters that MSFT, having risen so fast in so short a time, may now be poised for a reversal.

If your fears pan out and MSFT does in fact change direction and starts going south, you would lose the gains that you have already realized. In order to protect your profits you decide to get insurance against a drop in price by buying put options. Looking at the options chain (table) for MSFT you find that you can buy the 90 day strike 24 at a premium of $0.32. This means you are buying the right to sell the stock at a price of $24 and you have a period of 90 days to exercise your right, if you decide to do so. For this privilege of price protection you are paying the option seller a premium of $0.32 per share or a total of $160 for the entire 500 shares that you own. You now can sleep peacefully thinking that if MSFT's price starts dropping and continues to do so within the next 90 days, you are guaranteed to be able to sell your entire holding at the price of $24.00 no matter how low the price drops. Even as you are protected or insured against a price drop in your Microsoft stock you are still in the driver's seat if the stock continues its upward trend. You will continue to benefit from any price improvement since you still own the shares.

Now assuming the price started dropping as you had feared and at the end of the 90 period it is down to $19.80, you can then exercise your puts and sell the shares at the guaranteed price of $24.00. On the other hand if the stock continued its rise and is at $27.35 at the end of the 90 option period your put options would expire and you would then lose the $160 premium you paid for the protection. But this is a small price to pay for the security it gave you. Moreover, as the price is now $27.50 the additional gain you achieved more than offset the $160 loss. At this point you can once again sell puts to protect the new price of $27.50.

So far we have discussed the meaning and benefits of 'buying' calls and puts. So if one can buy calls and puts there must also be sellers of these options. What's in it for the sellers?

While a call option buyer receives the right but not the obligation to buy a stock at a specified price during a specified period of time, the call option seller has the obligation to sell the stock to the call option holder at the agreed price if the latter decides to exercise the call option on or before the option expires. In short, the call buyer's right gives him an alternative of exercising or not exercising his right to buy, while a call option seller has no alternative, he has an obligation to sell if the buyer exercises his right. Putting it yet another way, the option buyer acquires a right while the option seller takes on a potential obligation.

For example: You own 500 shares of stock in XYZ Company whose shares are currently trading at $45. You bought the stock several months ago when it was trading at $25. You are now in profit and you're afraid that if the price drops steeply you may lose the profit you've already gained. At the same time you are reluctant to sell your shares because you may give up the chance that XYZ's stock may continue to rise thereby denying yourself the opportunity for more profits. You are in a quandary of whether to take the risk of not selling and face the possibility the stock may soon start declining, or sell now and lose the potential for further profits if the stock continues its upward trend. You finally decide on a compromise of selling call options against your stock.

You go ahead and instruct your broker to sell 5 call option contracts at a contract price (strike price) of $48 with a validity of 90 days. You receive a premium of $2 for the calls you just sold for a total amount of $1,000 (5 contracts x 100 shares x $2). By this transaction of selling calls you placed yourself obligated to sell your XYZ stock to the call option buyer at the contract price of $48 for a period of 90 days. Let us say the stock price continues to climb and 50 days later when the price hits $54 the option holder decides to exercise his calls. He now compels you, the option seller, to sell your stock to him at the agreed contract price of $48. In this scenario both, you the option seller and the option buyer are winners to some degree. By selling call options you gave up the chance of gaining another $9 in profits when the stock climbed to $54 but you still gained $5 in the process, $2 from the sale of the options plus $3 when you sold the stock to the option holder at $48. The option buyer is a winner since he now buys the stock from you at $48 instead of the current priced of $54. His cost is $48 plus the $2 he paid for the call option for a total of $50. At this point he can then turn around and sell his stock at the current price of $54 and make a nice profit of $4 per share.

But as in the previous example, in the real world chances are the option buyer would most likely sell his options rather than exercise them if his intention is to make a profit. He would gain a larger profit selling his options than exercising them and then selling the stock.

Okay, now that we have seen how the Call option seller benefits let's see how the Put option seller makes out. As stated earlier a Put option buyer receives the right but not the obligation to sell stock. On the other side of the fence the put seller places himself in a position where he is obligated to buy the stock assigned to him by the put buyer should the put option buyer choose to exercise his right. The process whereby a put buyer exercises his right to compel the put seller to buy and take delivery of stock is called assignment. The put option holder is assigning his stocks to the put option seller.

Going back to the example of the XYZ Company whose stock is currently trading at $45, let's say you're interested in the stock but feel that $45 is a high price to pay for it. You would be willing to take a position in the stock if and when the price declined to what you think is a fairer value. In your opinion XYZ's share price should be around $40. But the market seems to be quite stable at this time and it may take a while before XYZ moved either up or down, hopefully down, since you would like to buy at a lower price. You have $12,000 in cash which you are prepared to commit for the purchase of 300 shares of XYZ stock at $40. While you are waiting for the market to move in your direction (lower) your cash is sitting idle in your brokers account and earning a pittance in interest, if at all. Meanwhile the stock price could continue staying at the present price range indefinitely, moving slightly up and down, without either gaining much or losing much. As a businessman/investor, you're thinking: "Hey this is not doing me any good. My money is tied up in my account earning hardly anything. This is not the way I envision myself making money in the stock market." You therefore decide to generate some income from your $12,000 cash fund by selling put options on XYZ Company.

You sell 3 put contracts (each contract equates to 100 shares) at a strike price (exercise price) of $40, the price that you are willing to pay for 300 shares of XYZ Company. The validity of the put option is 90 days and you receive a premium of $2 for the sold puts or a total of $600. The $600 is yours to keep whether or not the put option holder exercises the options. If at the end of 90 days, or on expiration date, XYZ stock is trading at say, $39, the option holder may assign his stock to you in which case you are compelled to purchase 300 shares of XYZ stock at $40 per share -- the contracted strike price. This is great for you because you are now purchasing the stock at the price you planned plus you have in your pocket $600 from the sale of the put options. In effect you are paying a net price of $38 ($40 less the $2 premium you received for the sold options) for stock that is now trading at $39.

Options allow stock investment for fraction of cost

Options are a great way for one to establish a position or acquire an interest in a stock for a fraction of the cost of buying the stock. This great leveraging power of options is the biggest draw for investors, and most especially speculators to the options trading game.

For example: Jonathan is attracted to buy stock in XYZ Company whose shares are currently priced at $65 each. He feels XYZ Company is poised for growth and its stock price has good potential to rise within the next two to four months. He wants to hold enough shares in the company to maximize his profit as and when the price increases. He believes the stock could go up to a high of around $85 per share eventually. However he only has $3,000 at his disposal to take a position in XYZ Company. With this amount he can only acquire 46 shares for a total entry investment of $2,990. If XYZ's stock does go up to $85 per share his 46 shares would have a value of $3,910 or a profit of $920. But Jonathan is hot on XYZ Company and he wants to hold more shares to cash in a bigger profit. He therefore decides to purchase call options on XYZ Company and he finds the right calls quoted at $2. Each option contract consists of 100 shares of the underlying stock. His $3,000 will therefore get him 15 contracts. This would enable him to acquire an interest or control 1,500 shares of XYZ Company – 15 contracts multiplied by 100 shares per contract. As you will learn later on, as the price of the underlying stock increases call options on the stock rise more aggressively than the stock price. The rate of increase is dictated by many factors, primarily by the price of the underlying stock, volatility in the market, speed of the increase, supply and demand as well as many other factors. Assuming that in six weeks the stock has risen to a price of $78 and his call option is now quoted at say, $3.50. Liquidating his position now would generate a cash inflow of $5,250 yielding him a profit of $2,250. If he had bought 46 shares of the stock instead of buying options and sold it at $78 his profit is a mere $598 instead of the whopping $2,250 with options. This is how the leveraging power of options makes it so attractive to investors and speculators.

Options Minimize investment risk

Options are an amazing tool to use as a hedge in stock investments. This feature of options was similarly illustrated in the previous examples of the farmer and wholesaler. Let's say that in the example above you purchased 300 shares of XYZ Company at $65 for a total cost of $19,500. The stock goes up to $78 and you are now tempted to sell and take your profits. But you find that the stock is still hot and would like to continue riding it for more profits if the price continues to rise. However, you are also afraid that something might suddenly happen to make the stock's price reverse in price and continue dropping considerably. What to do? As you learn more about options and the many ways to use them, you will find there are various alternatives available to you as protection from a declining market. For this exercise we will discuss the simplest of these alternatives and that is the buying of put options.

As in an earlier example of how puts can serve as insurance against loss of value in your investment, you buy put options which gives you the right to sell the stock at a predetermined price in case the market drops. This is a hedging strategy that minimizes or eliminates your risk of a lower price. In this example you do this by buying 3 put contracts which give you the right to sell 300 shares at the predetermined price of say, $75. The nearer the strike price is to the current market value of $78 the more expensive the puts will be. Let's say the $75 puts cost $1.50 each for a total of $450 for the 3 contracts (3 x 100 x $1.50). If the price drops to say,

$70 in the period that you are holding your puts, you can do either of two things. Exercise your right to sell the shares at $75 instead of the current $70 market price thus preventing yourself from losing the full $8 if you did not have the puts. In this scenario you would have given away only $6.50 instead of the full $8. Or you could sell your shares at the current price of $70 pocketing $21,000 and simultaneously sell your puts which at this time could be valued at much higher than the $1.50 you originally paid for it. Assuming the puts are priced at $3 this would get you another $900 which added to your $21,000 yields a total of $21,900. In either case using puts to hedge your position enabled you to cushion your loss of profits.

Options can offer extremely high returns

The ability of options to offer potentially very high returns for small capital invested is the biggest draw for the thousands of worldwide investors and traders who flock to options trading.

Let's go back to the earlier illustration where Jonathan used options to acquire an interest in XYZ Company whose stock was getting hot. In that example he bought 15 call contracts at the premium price of $2 when XYZ, the underlying stock, was trading at $65. Let's assume he bought call options with a strike price of 80. The 15 contracts cost him a total of $3,000 excluding broker's commissions and other fees. As the price of the underlying security, XYZ stock rises, so do the call options tied to it. This is not always the case but let's assume for this illustration that the price rise is speedy enough as to cause the options to rise correspondingly. Generally when a stock's price is climbing steadily and rapidly the call options rise but at a faster rate than the underlying stock. After six weeks of continuous climb the stock is at $78 and the 80 strike call options are now quoted at $3.85. Jonathan thinks the stock price has reached its high point and liquidates his call options, selling them at $3.85 and taking in $5,775. He just made a profit of $2,775 on this play for a return of 92.5%, nearly double his initial investment of $3,000. If he had used his $3,000 to purchase the stock instead of options he would have been able to purchase only 46 shares at $65 per share for a total investment of $2,990. Selling his stock at $78 would give him a mere $3,588 for a return of 20% on his invested capital of $2,990, far less than the 92.5% he achieved with his call options. This is the kind of scenario that hundreds of option web sites hype to the general investing public thus luring countless newcomers to what is peddled as a fantastic investment instrument. What these sites don't mention are the pitfalls that await the novice investor. More on this later.

Options offer dozens of strategic trading techniques suited for each investor's goal

Another great benefit of options is its ability to offer numerous investment alternatives. Owing to its very flexible nature options can be used in a multitude of ways to suit every investor's ultimate goal.

Investing directly in stocks limits the investor's ability to profit or loss in only two situations. He profits when the stock moves up and loses when the stock moves down. If his stock remains stagnant he neither wins nor loses so his investment is, so to speak, asleep and not producing returns. Except when he is invested in a dividend paying stock he may then draw some income out of his holdings, but it is nowhere near the rates of return that options could provide. With options, either alone or in conjunction with stocks, the investor is presented with a dizzying array of choices that enable him to position his investment in myriad ways to achieve his investment goals. Believe it or not there are dozens of different option strategies employed by traders and investors depending on how they want to position themselves. Using options allows an investor to make money even in a non directional market where stocks are neither moving up nor down. Out of the many strategies available the ones listed below are the more popular and most commonly used strategies.

- Long Call
- Long Put
- Protective Put
- Covered Call
- Cash Secured Put
- Naked calls
- Naked puts
- Bull Call Spread
- Bear Put Spread
- Debit call spread
- Credit call spread
- Debit put spread
- Credit put spread
- Calendar spreads
- Backspread
- Butterfly spread
- Ratio spread
- Vertical bull spread
- Vertical put spread
- Collar
- Long Straddle
- Long Strangle
- Iron condor

The list goes on and on. Many of the strategies are combinations of one or the other of the above or adaptations of several combinations. These are called spreads. To explain each and every strategy with corresponding trading illustrations would extend the length of this book to several volumes. It's enough to say that all the strategies have particular functions that deliver what an investor seeks. There are strategies that provide the elements for extremely high returns but the investor takes on much higher risks. On the other end of the spectrum there are those strategies that minimize the risk factor to hardly any, but the returns are extremely small. In between there are all the other strategies that enable the investor to achieve his goals.

In this book I have chosen to explain and illustrate the trading strategy that has worked well for me and one that can be used by investors as an investment technique to achieve consistent above average annual returns with manageable or nearly neglible risk. Before I proceed in taking the reader to the main topic in this book let us review some of the terms that are used in the illustrations.

CHAPTER TWO

Familiarizing yourself with option terms

The very last chapter of this book is a glossary of terms widely used in the options industry, many of which are used in this book. The Glossary section gives definitions of many option terms but I would like to bring up and explain some of the more frequently used language in this book's trading examples.

At-the-Money (ATM), In-the-Money (ITM) and Out-of-the-Money (OTM); Intrinsic Value and Extrinsic Value

These terms describe the position of the option's strike price in relation to the current market price of the underlying stock. In the table below we are looking at the option chains for Microsoft stock (symbol: MSFT) when the stock is currently trading at $24.80 and there is still many weeks left in the life of the options prior to expiration. The strike prices are listed in the center of the table. The numbers on the left are call option bid and ask premiums and those to the right are put option bid and ask premiums. The shaded areas are the call and put options that are in-the-money (ITM) and the unshaded areas are those that are out-of-the-money (OTM).

When we say that an option is ATM, it means that the strike price and the current market price of the stock ($24.80) are at parity or at the same price or very near the same price. In the table we can consider the call 25 strike as ATM since it is very near to the underlying's current price of $24.80. The same thing is true on the put side with the put 24 strike being close to the current price. As the strike price gets inside the current price of the stock it is said to be getting ITM. At the strike price of 24 the CALL option is $0.80 in-the-money (ITM). What this means is that the call option with strike 24 has a real or intrinsic value of $0.80 which is the difference between the market price and the strike price. Intrinsic value is the real value of an option.

In the case of calls shown in the table the options with strike prices lower than 25 all have intrinsic or real value as well as time value. If you are wondering why in the table the call option 24 has a bid price of 1.19 and ask of 1.21, both above the $.80 real value, the reason is time value or extrinsic value. Extrinsic value, the term used in options lingo, is the value assigned to the option for the remaining time left to expiration. At the bid price of $1.19 the call 24 has $0.80 of intrinsic value and $0.39 of extrinsic value. The lower the strike price of the call the higher is the bid and ask premiums because they are deeper ITM and therefore containing a higher intrinsic value. Strike prices higher than 25 have no intrinsic value. The quotes represent only time value or extrinsic value and therefore are called out-of-the-money options (OTM). The higher the strike price is from $24.80 the cheaper are the bid and ask premiums. This is because as the strike price moves farther upward it goes farther away from the stock's current price and therefore becomes more difficult for Microsoft's market price to go up to that level thereby becoming less attractive to investors, consequently commanding cheaper premiums.

MICROSOFT CORPORATION SYMBOL: MSFT PRICE: $24.80

	LAST	BID	ASK	STRIKE	LAST	BID	ASK	
ITM	5.25	4.85	4.90	20.00	0.05	0.03	0.04	OTM
ITM	4.20	3.85	3.95	21.00	0.06	0.05	0.06	OTM
ITM	3.17	2.93	2.96	22.00	0.10	0.09	0.10	OTM
ITM	2.08	2.01	2.03	23.00	0.16	0.17	0.18	OTM
ITM	1.22	1.19	1.21	24.00	0.32	0.35	0.36	ATM
ATM	0.57	0.56	0.58	25.00	0.71	0.72	0.74	ITM
OTM	0.23	0.21	0.22	26.00	1.34	1.38	1.39	ITM
OTM	0.08	0.07	0.08	27.00	2.06	2.20	2.25	ITM
OTM	0.04	0.03	0.04	28.00	3.20	3.15	3.20	ITM
OTM	0.03	0.02	0.03	29.00	3.93	4.15	4.20	ITM
OTM	0.02	0.01	0.02	30.00	5.05	5.15	5.20	ITM

In the case of puts the table shows a reverse picture. As you know a put gives you the right to sell stock but not the obligation. So if you own Microsoft stock and you are a holder of a Microsoft put option strike 25 you can sell your stock at $25 if you exercise your right to sell even if MSFT's current market price is $24.80. In this case the put option 25 is $0.20 ITM. The table shows bid and ask of .71 and .72 and here again, as in calls, the difference is time value or extrinsic value. Put option 25 therefore consists of $0.20 intrinsic value and $0.52 time value for a total of $0.72 on the bid price and $0.74 on the ask price. As the option strike goes higher than the market price the put option gets deeper ITM, increasing its intrinsic value and therefore commanding higher premium prices. Going the opposite direction, the lower the strike prices, the less intrinsic value they have or none at all, consisting only of extrinsic value. Again these options become less attractive to put option buyers thus commanding much less option premiums. They are said to be OTM options.

American Style versus European Style options

It's important to know if the options you choose to trade have American type or European type expiration. Most ETFs and stocks have American type expirations while many of the indexes are of the European type. What is the difference? Simply that American type options can be exercised any time before expiration while the European type can be exercised only on the date of expiration, not before. American options are advantageous to buyers while the European type are more beneficial to sellers. Let's look at how American type options benefit buyers.

You are given a tip that Microsoft stock, because its business has been quite good in the current year, is poised to make a dramatic rise in the coming months. The stock is currently trading on June 15, at $24.80. You do some investigation and believe there might be some truth to the rumors. You're still skeptical that it may take off as others believe and so instead of buying the stock now at $24.80 you look at buying call options on Microsoft with the intention that if indeed it starts rising and goes beyond your option strike price you could exercise your option and still buy Microsoft at less than market.

You proceed to buy 10 contracts of the OTM September 26 calls at a price of $0.22. Your total investment is $220. As the months go by Microsoft, true to rumors, start heading up and as August rolls around, and as it hits 29.50, it starts losing steam and goes on a steady trading pattern. You're now excited about owning Microsoft stock and the thought of being able to acquire it at only $26 (the strike price of your call options) when it's now trading at $29.50. You make a decision to act now and notify your broker that you would like to exercise your call options today and not wait till expiration on the third Friday of September. Since MSFT options are of the American type you are allowed to do so and immediately acquire ownership of 1000 shares of Microsoft stock (10 call contracts x 100) at $26 per share. Your total cost for the entire lot is $26,220 including the cost of the premium you paid for the original 10 call contracts. A few days later the stock resumes its upward climb and by the end of August it's trading at $33.00. At this price MSFT has now risen 33% in a very short period of time since you bought your call options. You feel that the stock is overpriced at this level. Fearing that it could undergo a sharp correction and pull back to below $33 per share you decide to liquidate your position and take your profits. Sure enough a week after you exited the market MSFT begun sliding down and by the middle of September, just about the time your original call options were expiring, the stock settled down at a price of $26.75. If you had not exercised your calls earlier, as you did, you would now be faced with the prospect of either buying the stock at $26, when the market is just a little higher at $26.75, or letting your options expire worthless.

If they were European type options, you couldn't have exercised your right in August to buy MSFT at $26 since you would have had to wait till expiration on the third Friday of September. You would have been locked in without an opportunity to exercise your options for the entire duration of the validity of the call contracts. You would have therefore missed the chance of buying the stock and selling it for a nice profit during those three months.

Now let's look at how European type options are more beneficial to option sellers. In the example above, if you were the seller of the calls instead of the buyer and assuming MSFT are of the American type options, you would have been compelled to sell the 1,000 shares of Microsoft at $26 per share when the call option holder exercised the options in August. At that time Microsoft was then trading at $29.50. As the seller of American type options you had to honor your obligation to sell even before the expiration date. If MSFT were of the European type the call option holder could not have exercise his options until expiration date in September and by that date the price had then dropped to $26.75. In all likelihood the call holder would not exercise his options in September when MSFT is at $26.75. In this example if MSFT had been a European type option you were not compelled to let go of your shares in August at $26 when MSFT was then at $29.50. As the option seller, you get to keep the premium that the holder paid you plus you continue to keep your 1,000 shares of Microsoft stock.

Option Pricing

Up until this time I've been talking about intrinsic value and time value--also called extrinsic value--as making up the price of an option. In reality there are many other factors that determine the price of an option. Like stocks, supply and demand comes very much into play. If there are more buyers than sellers the option will tend to increase in price and vice-versa, if there are more sellers than buyers the option will have downward price pressure. Then there is volatility which has a great impact on option pricing. Finally there is the dividend factor. If the underlying stock will be paying dividends during the life time of the option this will have an effect on the price of the option.

Volatility as a component of an option price

If I were to define volatility in its simplest form I would call it the market's emotional sentiment. Using the technical description of volatility as presented in books and manuals, it is the measure of stock price movement, or how much a stock price moves up and down. The greater the up-and-down movement of the stock, the greater is the insecurity of the players thus the more erratic the behavior of the underlying stock and the derivative option. Putting all the different elements that affect option pricing we can then say an option's price is a combination of:

intrinsic value + extrinsic value + volatility + dividend + the element of supply and demand. The first four elements can be calculated mathematically but the last element of supply and demand can only be determined at the trading floor.

Okay, so we have now covered the many benefits and advantages of using options as an incredible tool to enhance stock investments. Surely there must be some negatives to options. Of course there are. And there are three that stand out: (1) Complexity, (2) Time decay, (3) Unlimited Risk.

Options are complex financial instruments

Options can be very complex and can require extensive education on the part of investors and traders. That's why there are numerous books and teaching materials in the form of videos, web sites, blogs, option forums and what have you. I hope this book contributes to your learning process in making options easy, understandable and potentially profitable.

Time decay, the enemy of option traders

Only if you're an option buyer. Time decay is that characteristic of options to lose value as time elapses. Actually it is the extrinsic value that is diminishing, not the intrinsic value. When an option is OTM it only contains extrinsic value and time eats away at this value rapidly as it draws nearer its expiration date. If you are an option buyer, which is what the bulk of option traders are, for you to make money on your investment, the underlyng stock price must appreciate rapidly in the case of calls, or decline rapidly in the case of puts, in order to make up for the diminishing value of the option with the passage of time. This is the reason that time decay is listed as one of the big disadvantages of options. The time sensitive nature of options leads to the result that most options expire worthless thus losing money for those who bought them. While this is a disadvantage to option buyers, it is a big advantage to option sellers. The reason it's mentioned as a disadvantage is because there are far more option buyers than there are sellers. Whenever options are mentioned by anyone the first thing that comes to mind is buying a call or a put. Seldom do you hear people talking about selling options.

Unlimited risk

The third disadvantage of 'Unlimited Risk' applies only to those who employ the strategy of selling or writing uncovered or naked options. This supposed risk is similar to the risk of short selling stocks or commodities.

Except for the first disadvantage of options being complex instruments where one has to go through a learning curve, the other two are non issues to the trader who has learned the proper trading techniques in overcoming these negatives. This is what this book is all about.

The trading strategy outlined in this book teaches a very specialized method of using options by the investor who wishes to use it as an investment tool for long term capital appreciation. As already mentioned, trading strategies, techniques and trading systems available to the option trader are so numerous today that it would take several volumes to describe each strategy in great detail. It would be far beyond the scope of what could be covered in one book. There are now many books and web sites on options that attempt to cover some of the most common trading strategies but from what I've seen many of these favor the principle of buying calls and puts or, variations of this strategy such as the use of debit spreads. The reason for the popularity of buying calls and puts and its variations as has already been mentioned earlier and is really quite simple, limited or defined loss against the potential for unlimited and fabulous profits. This is what has driven thousands into the options trading game. But like everything else in life there is always a trade off. While the potential for fabulous profits against limited investment exists the reality of achieving such success is restricted. It's somewhat similar to buying a lottery ticket where one has the potential for winning fabulous riches against a very small investment in the cost of the ticket. Or putting it differently, it's also akin to going to a casino and placing bets on gaming tables with the hope that at the end of the evening you will come out with a lot more money than you came in. As we all know there are very few winners in casinos and that is why the gambling business offers tremendous profits for the operators.

But one can be an option trader and be in a similar position as the casino operator. How? By being an option writer or seller instead of a buyer. For every option that is bought in the market, there must be a seller or writer of the option. These writers are the casinos in the options business. As the option seller you take the bets from the option buyers and since 75 to 80 percent of all options in the market expire worthless, you the seller pocket the 'bets' or premiums paid by the buyers when the options they bought expire worthless. For the benefit of those who are not familiar with gambling casinos, the winning odds of casinos over the betting player is only around 5 percent and yet they rake in profits from this business. Now imagine this, research and studies have shown that the option writer (seller) has better than 10 to 20 percent odds over the option buyer.

Option traders who successfully use the strategy of selling options consider themselves as having found the Holy Grail of Investments. And of all the variations in option selling strategies (just as many as there are in option buying), writing naked or uncovered options is considered to be the Cadillac division. No other option selling system offers the profit potential of the naked writer.

So why aren't there more naked option writers in the market? For two reasons:

1. There is the general belief that writing naked options carries the potential for unlimited losses. This has served to scare away the thousands of novice traders and those who have not been long enough traders to recognize the benefits of option writing and the many safeguards available that conquers this so-called risk.

2. For many, options trading has become synonymous with making big profits quickly from small investments. Option sellers on the other hand, do not have the potential for outrageous profits from any single trade, and by not being a get-rich-quick proposition it is less popular to traders who are looking for big returns on their small investments.

It must be noted however, that option writing is fast gaining popularity among serious investors looking to grow their wealth at a steady, consistent and secure manner regardless of market or economic conditions. For those willing to venture into this lucrative field for long term capital appreciation don't let the first reason above frighten you into inaction. There are many ways you can protect yourself and conquer the element of 'unlimited losses' in writing nakeds. This book goes into much detail in describing one such method.

CHAPTER THREE

Options as an investment vehicle

It is a well known fact that serious investors seeking long term growth of capital have as their main objectives the two most basic goals in investing:

- to find an investment vehicle that would effectively preserve capital and minimize risk in the face of a fluctuating and constantly flexing world economy.
- the investment vehicle must provide better than decent yields in all economic conditions to promote constant growth of capital value.

With the stock market as the premiere choice due to its historical record of outperforming all other investments over time, people are increasingly turning to the stock market as their main investment vehicle for future capital growth. It is here where higher rates of return can be made with relatively controllable risk.

With thousands of books, manuals, internet sites, seminars and courses offering investment strategies and trading systems in the stock market and its derivatives, there are few, if any, that deliver the ideal investment vehicle sought by the long term investor in search of safety and above average returns. Not only is there a near total absence of an ideal investment system but there are many that promise eye popping, mind boggling returns and, they are exactly that; mere promises.

Many books and web sites are touting trading strategies in stocks and derivatives that supposedly deliver stellar returns. Most of these trading systems are structured on strategies or activities that work when conditions are ideally suited to the program being peddled. Most of their successes are highly dependent on picking the right stocks at the right time, with the market moving in the right direction in the right amount of time. In other words you must be a good stock picker to select the right ones consistently. Market timing is also an important factor in their systems. Again, you must be a good market timer to be correct all the time and this is almost an impossibility. These supposedly high yield investment programs don't say anything about how bad things can be when conditions go against their predictions. These programs do exactly as promised: great when the going is good but disastrous when the going is bad.

While there is no one investment system that can be an answer-all to the various goals of various investors, there are some investment alternatives that can come close to satisfying the two basic needs of safety and decent returns. Diversified mutual funds have been touted as the answer to these basic needs. But over the years these funds have shown that during downturns in the economy they perform just as badly as the whole investment market in general. And, over the long term, many of these diversified funds have failed to even match market performance in general, much less outperform it.

Enter market derivatives with emphasis options.

Trading in stock options has become very popular with institutional investors as well as private individuals as a sound money management system supplementing their investment portfolios. The ability of stock options to give the investor a wide range of choices is what has made the options market grow considerably over the last two decades. To quote one options expert: "Stock options are the greatest wealth producing tool ever invented on this planet. . . . if you know how to use them".

The key element of this statement is: "if you know how to use them"

For many serious investors (as opposed to speculators) looking for a safe haven for their money, the mere mention of stock options, sends shivers up their spine. They look at options as synonymous with great risk. But isn't driving a car very dangerous for one who doesn't know how to drive? The ability of stock options to give the investor a wide range of choices in stock market investments is what has made the options market grow by leaps and bounds over the last twenty years. Statistics compiled by the Options Industry Council, a group that educates investors about options, show that volume in options trading has risen tremendously in recent years. Further, studies show that individual investors make up 60% of the market.

For the individual who has sufficient funds and is looking for more than a decent return on his capital and with controllable risk, stock options may be the answer.

There are dozens of option trading systems being employed by individual investors and institutions. Each system is designed to accomplish a specific investment goal. Of the dozens of option trading systems there is one that can be carried out as a long term investment program offering a fair degree of safety and consistent high returns over time, thus satisfying the investor's two basic needs of safety and return.

This is the selling of uncovered or naked options.

But wait! Is it not said that selling naked options carries the risk of unlimited losses? Isn't this a contradiction?

Indeed selling naked options when done carelessly and without a disciplined strategic program is extremely risky!

But by using a carefully planned and disciplined system of trading, the so-called "unlimited risk" factor in selling options can easily be conquered. I have a three-pronged trading strategy that is proving to be a consistent winner in all market conditions. It is a trading technique that couples naked option selling with a modified ratio credit spread and the use of the roll over feature. While naked option selling has acquired a bad rap of being highly risky, this three-pronged trading strategy allows the trader to defeat the risk. Not only is the system able to substantially reduce the risk, it also offers one the ability to become a savvy investor/trader without having to depend on picking the right stocks or timing the market.

It involves utilizing the system in any market condition using only a few stocks, ETFs or indexes (the latter two are more effective). One need not worry about finding the right stocks or timing the trades. The fact remains that stocks behave, more often than not, in crazy and irrational ways so that one can almost say that consistently choosing winning stocks is nearly an impossible task. Rather than be proactive and try to predict and time the market, as many try to do, this three-pronged investment system is reactive. The prescribed trades are done in reaction to how the market has moved, not in anticipation of its future behavior.

This three-pronged trading system does not promise quick profits or mind boggling yields but steady annual returns in excess of 30%. It would be prudent to say that in times of deep downturns such as the deep market downturns of the early 2000s and those of 2008-2009 the system may not deliver the promised returns and may even result in losses, but it will certainly hold its own over the long term.

Risk Of 'Unlimited Loses' In Naked Option Selling Is A Myth!

The investment system described in this book is based on the strategy of selling naked or uncovered stock options, both calls and puts. For those who are already trading naked options successfully it is disconcerting for them to hear people say that selling naked options is extremely risky because it carries the threat of 'unlimited loses'. Nothing is farther from the truth! It's a myth!

While theoretically the selling of naked options carries with it the "potential" for unlimited loses, in the real world this so-called risk is controllable to such a large degree as to be meaningless. Thousands of option sellers are successfully making a good living and growing their capital doing nothing but sell naked options. The fact is all these successful traders are employing certain safeguards or protective trading techniques that allow them to defeat this 'unlimited risk' factor.

Those who mistakenly believe that naked option selling has the potential for 'unlimited loses' are obviously misguided in their belief. Selling or writing naked options when done in a disciplined manner coupled with proper protective trading techniques and sound money management is no riskier than buying options. Seasoned options traders who specialize in naked writing regard option buying as a riskier, more speculative trading strategy. Statistics show there are more traders who lose money as option buyers than option sellers.

Options are decaying assets. They lose value each day that the underlying stock to which they are attached remains unchanged or moves in a negative direction. The magnitude of daily losses depends on many factors but the primary one being the behavior of the underlying stock or index. As an option buyer (versus an option seller) you are faced with this dilemma and can only be a winner if you correctly determine the movement of the stock and the magnitude of the move. If the market moves in the opposite direction or if it does not move at all, you're a loser. The option buyer must not only correctly foretell market direction but your prediction must be accompanied by a major move in that direction. A less than significant move will still result in a loss. On the other hand, the option seller takes maximum advantage of the decaying characteristic of options. As an option seller you merely sit and wait for the option to lose value daily to the point of being worthless on expiration day. You don't need to correctly predict market direction to generate profits. If you sell puts, you're a winner if the stock stays flat, a winner if the stock goes up. You can only lose if the underlying drops far enough to hit past your strike price position. And even if the stock goes down you're still a winner if the move is not far enough to hit your strike position. If you're a call seller, you win when the stock drops, stays flat or moves up less than significantly. Admittedly, during the validity period of the option until its expiration date, you face the potential threat that the underlying stock may move continuously against you past your strike position, in which case there would be no limit to your loses. But this can only happen if you are careless enough not to watch and monitor your position on a regular basis.

Trading techniques that cancel the risk in naked options

Options are not 'buy and hold' securities. All options traders, buyers and sellers alike, carefully watch their positions on a regular frequency. In their march towards expiration dates options are always in motion in tandem with their underlying stocks thereby continuously presenting opportunities for making profits or presenting danger signals for incurring losses. Option sellers are a more cautious lot than buyers and consequently sellers have developed various protective trading techniques to offset the so called 'unlimited risk' factor to the point where it is nearly a negligible risk. What are these trading techniques? Each option seller may have his own system but here are a few strategies that offset the risk:

1. First and foremost and probably the most important thing to consider when getting into selling options is the choice of securities. Highly volatile stocks are most susceptible to the highest risks because of their potential for mak-

ing dramatic price moves up or down. While volatile stocks tend to offer attractive option premiums, this benefit can be cancelled by the higher risk of a major negative move. A price gap out in a stock can cause severe losses. Conservative option sellers who make a living or grow their wealth selling options will often tend to trade ETFs (Exchange Traded Funds) or Indexes instead of stocks. These securities seldom undergo dramatic one day moves and it is even less vulnerable to price gap outs.

2. Careful monitoring of position – As mentioned earlier, option sellers tend to be a cautious lot and anyone who sells options and does not watch the progress of his position can only be considered dumb or stupid. One does not need to be glued to his computer screen and watch every move in the stock market. You only need a cursory look at the market now and then to see how things are developing. When a situation starts building up where your short position may be in danger, action can immediately be initiated before it degenerates into a bad situation. The option sold may be bought back immediately at a slight loss before it gravitates to bigger losses. This slight loss can be no more than what an option buyer would be exposed to in a similar negative scenario. And this is assuming you, the option seller, do nothing more than buy back the losing position. But if your monitoring is combined with the other strategies illustrated below then the risk of loss is nearly nil.

3. Use of stop losses – For the trader who does not have the time to occasionally watch the market you may use stop losses on your positions at the same time that you initiate the short positions. I believe there is no need to explain here what a stop loss is as it is presumed anybody who is in the stock and options market knows what this is. Additionally, with the advent of online trading, electronic alerts can be initiated with brokers so that when a perilous situation starts

developing an automatic alert signal is sent to the trader's email, iphone, or cell phone.

4. Use of credit spreads – Rather than go into a long explanation of what credit spreads are, and I'm sure many of your already know what this is, I will hold off talking about it until later. This is actually one of the techniques used in the options selling strategy discussed later in this book.

5. Use of the roll-out feature – This is one strategy that is not being used to maximum advantage by many option traders. Based on their personal trading experiences and extensive use of this feature those who have been using it swear by it as a powerful defensive strategy in preventing losses in option selling.

Strategy number 5 above is effective enough when used alone and by itself, but when combined with the other strategies above, the whole system becomes a formidable program that almost totally eliminates losses in option selling

For those who are contemplating of getting into the option selling business, pay no heed to the naysayers. Next time you hear someone say "naked option selling is extremely risky due to the potential for unlimited losses" that person is most likely an option buyer who has never ventured into the lucrative field of option selling. His remark obviously comes from his ignorance of the inner workings of options and the various safeguards available to the option seller. To the knowledgeable option seller the risk of losing money is less than the risk facing the option buyer.

Option Rollouts – What are they?

I mentioned option rollouts in the previous section as one of the best safeguards available to the option seller in protecting against risk. For those who have not yet discovered the benefits of rolling out options, it's high time you look closely at this very valuable feature. Roll outs not only offer additional profit generating advantages but more importantly it offers an extraordinary ability for limiting or eliminating potential losing positions. Before going on to describe the remarkable benefits of using the rollout process let's be sure you understand what is meant by rolling out an option. It is simply the closing of one option position and the opening of another position either farther away in strike price or farther away in expiration date, or both, with the objective of transforming an existing precarious condition into a more beneficial one.

There are many situations where option rollouts may be used. I will just touch on two of the more practical uses of the rollout process. The first is the benefit it gives the covered call player. The second is the remarkable ability of the rollout feature to offer protection against the potential for loss that faces the naked option writer.

Benefit of rollouts to covered call option traders

Consider this scenario: you own 500 shares of XYZ Company which you originally bought some time back at a price of $50 per share. It is now June 12 and the market has recently gone on an uptrend so that your XYZ stock has appreciated to $60. You are tempted to sell and take in profits from your investment. At the same time you don't want to miss out on any further upward movement the stock may take in the face of what appears to be a strengthening market. Yet you are also afraid that the market might reverse direction and you could then lose some of the profits you've already realized. In this instance you may want to do a covered call option trade, that is, selling call options against your stock. This enables you to participate in any future appreciation of your stock, and the cash generated from the option sale serves as profit at the same time providing some protection if the market should change direction forcing you to exit your position.

Okay, so your stock is now at $60 and you sell 10 contracts of the August 64 (strike) call options at a premium of $0.62. Your 500 shares would generate $310 in premium from the sale of the 10 contracts. The stock continues gaining momentum and on July 15 the price is at $64. Your August 64 calls are now ATM (at-the-money) and could be exercised by the option holder. At this point you are faced with two nice choices. Let the option holder call the options (exercise his right to buy the stock at the strike price of $64) or, roll out the options to a farther expiration and higher strike price allowing you to participate in further gains if the stock continues its upward trend. If you let your options be called you have gained not only the money from the option sale ($310) but also from the appreciation price of the stock, now at $64 when at the time you sold your call options it was at $60. But it would be a pity to have your August 64 options called and you are forced to sell your stock at $64 when it looks very likely that XYZ will continue to rise in price. A roll out of your August 64 calls would take you out of the current dilemma. After much deliberation you elect to roll out your August 64 calls to a farther expiration and higher strike price. In so doing you continue to participate in the uptrending game.

You proceed and buy to close the August 64 calls at say, $1.15. The option ask price has gone up in tandem with the underlying stock's rising price. At the same time you sell a new set of 10 contracts of the November 68 calls at a premium of $1.60. With most options brokers you can do these two trades simultaneously as a spread order thereby reducing the broker's commission since it is treated as one single trade instead of two (see example of a spread trade order form below). This transaction has removed the potential threat of exercise on your August 64 calls by moving the strike price up to 68 and at the same time, with the expiration now far away in November, it gives XYZ stock the opportunity to continue rising and hopefully get up to $68 between now and November. If it does then you are again faced with the same two nice choices of letting your options be exercised at $68 or once again rolling it out to a farther expiration and a higher strike price. You can keep doing this for as long as there are far out expiration dates to roll out to.

SAMPLE OF A ROLL-OUT ORDER DONE AS A SPREAD TRADE

The transaction below shows the closing of the April 82 puts and rolling them out to the June 79 puts for a credit of $0.96 thereby generating a positive cash flow of $960. The trade was done when IWM was trading at $82.22

Symbol				Action	Quantity
IWM	Apr11	82	Put	Buy To Close	10
Find Chain					
Symbol				Action	Quantity
IWM	Jun11	79	Put	Sell To Open	10
Find Chain					

Price
- Market
- Limit/Credit* $ .96
- Limit/Debit* $
- Even

Duration: Day Order

	Last	Bid	Ask
IWM	82.22	82.21	82.36
IWM Apr11 82 Put	1.67	1.61	1.67
IWM Jun11 79 Put	2.64	2.63	2.71

Quotes as of 3/27/2011 5:55:14 PM ET

Benefit of rollouts to naked option sellers

Now let's see how the roll out benefits the naked option writer. When you sell a naked option, be it call or put, you theoretically face the risk of unlimited losses in your position due to the fact that if the underlying security moves against you the potential for loss is unlimited. The term "theoretical risk" is used here because this risk has been blown out of proportion and grossly exaggerated. While the potential risk of loss does exist it's a negligible one if you employ appropriate strategies to defeat it. Please see section above Risk of 'Unlimited Loses' In Naked Option Selling Is A Myth where it talks about this theoretical risk being totally controllable using proper defensive strategies. One of the defensive strategies mentioned there is the use of roll outs.

Here's a scenario that may face an option writer. Let us suppose you sold naked puts several strikes OTM with expiration sixty days away. Sometime during its life the market turns against you and begins to drop down to the price level of the strike you sold. Many option traders would just close out the position buying back the puts at a higher price and taking a loss. You being the smart trader would roll out your puts by buying them back at the now higher price and at the same time sell new puts farther out in time and several strikes OTM, either at a higher price than you bought back your puts or at least at the same price you bought the closing puts. You've just converted your original 60 day puts into longer expiration puts with a higher strike price thereby avoiding taking a loss at this point in time. Just like the roll out of call options this process of closing and opening put positions can be done as a spread trade and in this way you are paying reduced broker's commissions.

If the market continues its downward trend you can keep rolling out your positions repeatedly till you reach a point where there are no more available future options to roll out to. At this point your puts may be so far out in the future that even if they go deep in the money chances of them being exercised are slim.

If you are going to be an option trader or already are one, rolling out is a must strategy in many of your option trades. You will find the strategy highly rewarding and in many cases offers a wide variety of choices to your trading styles. Not only does it enable you to increase your trading profitability but more importantly it affords you the ability to protect your trade positions against certain adverse conditions.

Is Option Selling The Holy Grail Of Investments?

While there is no such thing as the perfect investment vehicle, or the holy grail of investments, option sellers feel that option selling probably comes closest to it.

Let's take a look and see what exactly is regarded as an ideal investment.

When asked to define what the ideal investment is investors have various versions of what they consider to be the ideal investment or the Holy Grail of Investments. In the ultimate analysis, most investors feel that an ideal investment should provide the following qualities: safety of capital, consistent above average returns, immunity from economic and market fluctuations and finally, liquidity, or availability of funds should the investor find an immediate need to tap his resources. Safety of capital and high returns seem to be the most desirable of all yet these two are totally opposing factors in any investment. As the saying goes, the higher the risk, the greater the reward or inversely, the lower the risk the smaller the reward.

That said let's explore our choices. Until the advent of options there appeared to be nothing that came even close to being called an ideal investment let alone be called the Holy Grail of Investments. We had to face the fact that investment instruments were either low risk low reward or high risk high reward. Some investment instruments were somewhere in the middle ground but few or none were in the Holy Grail category. Investors may be classified into two groups, passive and active investors. Passive investors prefer entrusting their capital to third parties and doing nothing more than expect returns from their investments either on a regular basis or value appreciation over time. They put their money into a fixed return instrument such as passbook savings accounts, money market funds, treasury bills, certificates of deposits, bonds and included in this lot are dividend paying stocks and mutual funds. Then there are the other passive investors that prefer to place funds into long term appreciation assets with capital growth as their main goal. Examples of these types of investments would be real estate, precious metals, arts and antiques. All these investment instruments while delivering small returns on a year-on-year basis do offer much safety of capital.

The active investor on the other hand is a more adventurous individual. He seeks high returns for his money, hopefully at reduced risk, by actively being involved in trading the markets, be it real estate, stocks, bonds, commodities, futures, foreign exchange, options or whatever else can be traded and made money on. Although more of a risk taker he nevertheless tries to moderate his risk exposure by restraining his profit objectives or rates of return on his capital. While passive investors are happy with annual returns of 3 to 8 percent, active investors seek higher rates of over 12 percent and more like in the region of 14 to 18 percent per annum. Is this doable? Yes it is and many are happy actively trading the markets and achieving these returns using their own trading techniques that somewhat controls risk to an acceptable degree. Now here's the shocker. Option traders are able to generate annual profits in excess of 20 percent without exposing themselves to any more risk than those achieving 14 percent. Now here is an even greater shocker. Among those that trade options the ones specializing on the selling side generate annual returns in excess of 30 percent with many averaging annual returns in the region of 40 to 50 percent!

Foreign currency traders as well as commodities and futures traders sneeze at this claim saying that they can outshine the option seller in annual returns. True. But can they claim to do so at the same risk level as the option sellers? Highly unlikely!

Selling options (stocks, commodities, futures, etc) has become for many the Holy Grail of Investments. To the experienced option seller this trading strategy offers high, consistent, returns, a fair degree of immunity against economic and market fluctuations, liquidity, and finally safety of capital. This last claim may be open to debate from non-believers in this trading strategy. To be fair let's qualify the safety claim by saying that the inexperienced option seller is open to potentially heavy losses if he does not know what he is doing. But to the seasoned trader selling options is a safe investment strategy delivering all the qualities of an ideal investment to the point where successful option sellers claim to have found what to them is the closest one will ever get to the Holy Grail of Investments.

Selling options on stocks, which is the specialty of this writer, can be particularly rewarding using a carefully planned trading system combined with disciplined money management and with proper safeguards in place. There are many trading strategies in selling options. Some are simple enough, like the covered call technique, delivering fairly decent returns while others are more complex but more rewarding. There is one option selling system used widely by this writer that can be carried out as a long term investment program offering a fair degree of safety and delivering consistent high returns time after time. By using a carefully planned, three-pronged system of trading, the risks associated with selling options can easily be overcome.

CHAPTER FOUR

Cash Secured Put Selling as a conservative investment strategy

In the next chapter we will start immersing ourselves in the main subject of this book which is the trading system that I find to be the most rewarding investment strategy for annual returns that will grow capital steadily and consistently. But before going to that chapter and start talking about the merits of naked options I would like to touch on a trading style that should prove interesting for investors who have idle cash they could make good use of. Being that this book is about how options are a great tool for building wealth it is only fitting that I should include a chapter on one specific use of options to generate a steady income flow at minimal risk to the investor. The strategy involved in this option trade activity is the selling of puts against a cash position or what is termed in the industry as cash secured put selling. In this approach one makes use of cash to serve as security for selling what would otherwise be naked puts. This trading technique works well for people or institutions that have a fair amount of cash lying idle in an account that is not generating much income or they have it parked in a low interest account. In this group can be found money market funds, savings accounts, trust funds, pension funds, funds of investment clubs, etc.

Example: Nathan has $30,000 in cash deposited in a money market account earning 3.5% annual interest. He is already well invested in several mutual funds, some stocks, and has a comfortable balance in his 401K account to take care of his future retirement needs. He has a secured job and his salary is more than sufficient to cover all of his family's affluent lifestyle. He does not need to touch any of his investments to augment his daily living needs. He also has some money in a savings account for immediate emergencies.

Nathan feels that his $30,000 in the money market fund could be put to better use and generate a better return than the current meager interest he is getting. A friend tells him about options and how this amazing investment tool could in fact offer extraordinary returns for his dormant $30,000 fund. Nathan is astounded by what he hears from his friend and decides to study and learn more about stock options. In his learning activities he voraciously reads everything about options, attends seminars, visits web sites and joins discussion forums about options and the numerous strategies available to investors. He is initially overwhelmed by the complexities of some of the option trading systems and being that he is one who is loath to put any amount of money at even the smallest risk he decides that selling options is the best method to maximize returns on his $30,000. He has read that selling puts and calls when accompanied by a disciplined system of money management is the best way to go. Following the advice he gleaned from all the teaching materials and meetings his first move is to find a broker that specializes in option trading. He withdraws his $30,000 from his money market fund and opens an account with an options broker. He now has $30,000 sitting in his account and is ready to start trading.

Nathan knows that the easiest way to get into the options game is to just simply buy calls or puts or what is termed taking a long position in a call or a put. But from all that he has learned in his studies he also knows that simply buying calls or puts is nearly equivalent to placing your bet on a number at a roulette table in a casino. His chances of losing his investment in his long option position is about 80%. He finds the odds extremely unfavorable for a non gambler like him. But by being a seller instead of a buyer of options, he places himself on the opposite side of the table and therefore has an 80% chance of winning which he finds acceptable. Moreover, his findings from his various studies indicate that this 80%

favorable odds can be improved further when coupled with other techniques such as the rolling out routine. Also by being well disciplined and patient one can very nearly eliminate the risk of loss.

After looking and studying all the option selling strategies and, as Nathan is a cautious person with his money, he finds that the strategy of selling cash secured puts will work best for him even though the returns may be somewhat less than other more complex option strategies. Being new in the options game he seeks a more simple trading system and chooses to engage in selling puts against his cash position. He goes ahead and ventures into the put selling game. Knowing that selling puts on a stock may carry the potential for being assigned the stock if the put gets ITM at expiration, he chooses a stock or ETF that he would not mind owning in case this happens. Again, being cautious as he is, he figures that an ETF issue that mimics a basket of securities representing an industry or market sector would be safer than a stock. An ETF would not be subject to the whims and vagaries of the performance of a particular stock and would not be subject to an analyst's prognostications that may cause the stock to fluctuate wildly. By selling puts on an underlying ETF he feels comfortable that the underlying's price would not gyrate as could an individual stock. After studying dozens of available ETFs he selects the iShares Russell 2000 Index Fund which mimics the Russell 2000 Index. The stock symbol is IWM.

It is March 13 and IWM stock is trading on this day at $81.43. Looking at the option chain below Nathan proceeds to write 3 contracts of the May 78 puts at $1.88 and collects $564 in premium (3 x 100 shares per contract x $1.88). The 3 put contracts are fully secured by his $30,000 cash account. In fact he only needs $23,400 to secure the puts and since he received $564 from the sale his net investment to secure this transaction is $22,836. So as long as the stock price remains above 78 all the way to the third Friday of May, Nathan, as the option seller, is removed from the possible obligation of assignment or having to buy the stock at $78.

	CALLS				PUTS			
	Last	Bid	Ask	Strike	Last	Bid	Ask	
	10.62	12.75	12.85	**69**	0.43	0.43	0.44	
	11.4	11.83	11.93	**70**	0.53	0.51	0.52	
	10.65	10.93	11.03	**71**	0.61	0.61	0.62	
	9.8	10.05	10.14	**72**	0.74	0.73	0.74	
	8.31	9.17	9.27	**73**	0.87	0.86	0.87	
ITM CALLS	8.36	8.34	8.41	**74**	1.01	1.02	1.03	
	7.6	7.53	7.57	**75**	1.2	1.19	1.2	OTM CALLS
	6.78	6.73	6.76	**76**	1.4	1.39	1.41	
	6.18	5.96	5.98	**77**	1.63	1.62	1.63	
	5.26	5.21	5.23	**78**	1.88	1.88	1.89	
	4.56	4.51	4.52	**79**	2.17	2.17	2.18	
	3.88	3.84	3.85	**80**	2.5	2.5	2.51	
	3.25	3.21	3.22	**81**	2.87	2.86	2.87	
CURRENT STOCK PRICE →				81.43				
	2.67	2.63	2.64	**82**	3.29	3.28	3.3	
	2.11	2.1	2.11	**83**	3.76	3.76	3.77	
	1.65	1.64	1.65	**84**	4.3	4.3	4.31	
	1.29	1.24	1.25	**85**	4.9	4.9	4.91	
OTM PUTS	0.92	0.91	0.93	**86**	5.59	5.56	5.58	
	0.68	0.65	0.66	**87**	6.57	6.29	6.39	ITM PUTS
	0.44	0.45	0.46	**88**	7.1	7.07	7.18	
	0.3	0.3	0.31	**89**	8.45	7.91	8.03	
	0.2	0.19	0.2	**90**	9.25	8.79	8.91	
	0.13	0.12	0.13	**91**	10.05	9.46	9.83	
	0.07	0.07	0.08	**92**	12.42	10.63	10.85	

For this 60 day placement he will be getting a return of around 2.5% on his $22,836 investment which if annualized works out to about 16% interest. This is certainly a far cry from the 3.5% annual interest he is currently getting from his money market placement.

Now let's look at what possible downside there could be for Nathan. The only downside facing Nathan, if you can call this a downside at all, is the obligation to purchase 300 shares of IWM at $78 per share. Let's assume that a few weeks after he sold his puts IWM stock drops to $78, Nathan's strike price. At this point he could be assigned the stock even before expiration since IWM carries American style expiration (see Chapter 2). He changes his mind about buying the stock at $78 and chooses instead to roll his options farther out and in this way he gets out of possible assignment for the moment thereby giving him another opportunity to buy the stock at a later date at a lower price and at the same time continue to hold on to his revenues from sale of puts.

Suppose that the $78 level for IWM is reached sometime in the middle of April. The May 78 put that he originally sold at $1.88 now has an ask price of $2.50. He buys the May 78 puts at $2.50 to close the position and rolls out to August 74 puts. He sells 3 August 74 puts at $2.95 thus gaining another $0.45 in the roll out, or $135. He is again out of danger of being assigned and now has the opportunity to buy IWM stock at a lower price of $74 per share.

If due to unseen circumstances the stock market as a whole keeps on going down and IWM stock with it, Nathan can go on rolling out his positions. With some stock issues and ETFs, IWM being one of them, there are future options contracts that are as far as two years away. Since Nathan's original $30,000 funds in the money market was not something that he needed to use he would be happy if in the end, after having done several roll outs, he ends up buying IWM stock at a super low price of maybe in the region of $70 or less per share. He could then wait out a market rebound which would put his investment at a terrific position for appreciation.

There are also those stock investors who use cash secured puts for another reason. That is, to purchase stocks at less than market price. Assuming you wish to purchase Microsoft shares and the stock is currently trading at $24.80. You want to pay less for it but while you're waiting for that opportunity you would like to generate some income out of your idle cash. So you decide to sell puts with the end in view that if the stock does not decline to a lower price level you would still be generating income from your cash position. You proceed to sell puts with strike price $24 and get $0.35 premium. The stock maintains its price level and at expiration is trading at $23.80. At this point assignment could occur. If you allow assignment, you would now be buying the stock at $24 but your net cost is $23.65 ($24 less put premium of $.35). You have just bought Microsoft stock at a discount from its original price of $24.80 when you first decided you wanted the stock. And if the stock's price did not drop down to $23.80 but stayed at its present level of $24.80 there would be no assignment and your strike 24 put options would expire worthless allowing you to pocket the $0.35 premium as income on your cash account.

This chapter wouldn't be complete if I don't touch on the subject of what is the equivalent of cash secured puts on the call side. It is the writing or selling of calls against stock one owns and this is termed covered call writing. In effect you are selling calls with the guarantee that if the option is exercised you have the stock and can deliver the shares to the buyer. This is one of the more popular and one of the simpler trading strategies in generating income from stock you own. It's like paying yourself dividends on the stock. It is also the strategy to use if and when a cash secured option seller ends up being assigned stock. Here is how it works.

Richard owns 1000 shares of Intel Corporation (stock symbol INTC) which he bought a few years back at $12.74. Intel is now trading at $20.37 but Richard has decided to hold on to his stock in the belief that it has a good potential for further future growth. At the same time he is thinking that at today's current price his investment is worth $20,370 which is good. After conversations with his broker and others he finds that Intel's potential future growth may not be as robust as it has been in the past two years that he has owned it. Intel does not pay dividends to its shareholders so there is no prospect of earning income in this area. He could cash out now but then he will have to face the problem of where to invest the cash that will give him more than the measly money market rates of 3%-4% annual interest.

Richard consults his friend Nathan, who is an option seller, and asks him what he could do in the field of options to generate some income similar to what Nathan does.

Nathan tells him: "Richard, you are in a great situation where you could make the most from trading options."

"How so?" asks Richard.

"Well, you already own stocks that you acquired dirt cheap. So why not pay yourself dividends from the stock you own by selling options against it? As you know I'm an option seller, but I'm what is referred to as a seller of 'cash secured put options' since I don't own the stocks on which I sell put options against, but I have the cash to cover my sold positions in case the puts are called in. In your case you could be a covered call seller as you do have the stocks to cover your sold options. You would then be called a covered call option player. As such you could be generating a steady stream of cash from your Intel stocks."

"Okay, so how exactly does this thing work?"

Nathan responds: "Call your broker and tell him that you wish to sell call options against your Intel stock and he will walk you through the entire process"

Richard takes Nathan's advice and contacts his broker the following day. After his broker explained the whole process of how to do covered call writing Richard proceeds with selling options on his Intel holdings.

It is the first day of April, Richard looks at the Intel option chains and decides to sell 10 contracts of the July 22 call which is quoted at a bid price of $0.38. He sold 10 contracts because that equates to 1,000 shares of stock that he owns. The options expire on the third Friday of July, or about 90 days away. At the premium of .38 he generates a total cash inflow of $380. He just paid himself a dividend of $380 from his Intel shares. If in July Intel's price remains below $22.00 the call options Richard sold would surely not be exercised and he is then able to keep his stock as well as the $380 cash he got. He can then start the whole process and sell new call options 60 to 90 days away and once again generate another cash inflow from the sale. He can keep doing this every two or three months and it would be like paying himself quarterly dividends on a stock that does not officially pay dividends. Of course if Richard owned another stock that paid dividends like General Electric, he could still do the same thing of selling call options thereby augmenting the dividend rate paid by GE.

Now what happens in the event that Richard's call options go ITM and the calls are exercised? Assuming in the above example that Intel went on a rise and before expiration in July Intel's stock is trading at $24.20. His calls are exercised and he has to deliver his 1,000 Intel shares at the contracted price (strike price) of $22 per share. He then received the cash proceeds of $22,000. Add to this the original $380 he got from the sale of the calls and he ends up with a total of $22,380. With this much cash in hand he turns to his friend Nathan again and asks how he could play the puts selling game. Nathan then explains to Richard the mechanics of cash secured put selling.

One last point to consider before we leave this chapter is that the cash secured option writer is able to enhance his investment returns with just a minor twist on this strategy. This is by selling more put options than is covered by his cash fund. He could sell as much as 50 percent more options and he would still theoretically be covered entirely by his cash balance. How?

With very few exceptions all stock brokers allow clients to purchase stocks paying only one half of the market value of the stock. One who buys 1,000 shares of Intel stock at $20.37 would not have to pony up the entire amount of $20,370. He only needs to put up $10,185 for the entire 1,000 shares of Intel. Therefore as an option writer you could sell 11 contracts of Intel put strike 19 at $0.38 premium even if you only have $10,450 cash in your broker's account. Actually you would need only $10,032 to make the trade happen since you are receiving $418 from its sale thus increasing your total cash account to $10,450. In the event that the put options expire ITM and you are assigned the stock, you would buy the 1,100 shares at $19 per share but you would only be required to put up 50% of the total value or just $10,450. But if the puts expired worthless the $418 premium you got represents a return of 4.2% on your invested funds of $10,032. Assuming this whole episode happened in 90 days this return translates into an annualized yield of approximately 17%.

CHAPTER FIVE

The Modified Credit Ratio Spread

As stated in the previous pages the option trading system discussed in this book is recommended for those who have little desire to devote time to studying fundamentals, technicals and other factors that affect the stock market and the securities industry and its derivatives. Furthermore, the methods described here are based on trading stock or equity options but could possibly be used as effectively for those who intend to do trading in commodity futures options. Assuming that at this point you now possess good familiarity with options as they relate to underlying stocks, you should know then there are three ways a stock may behave which will eventually affect the values of the corresponding options. The stock price may go up, it may come down or, stay flat and not move at all. The options tied to the underlying stock pretty much follow the same actions. Of these three, the naked put seller (assuming you are selling puts) is a winner if the stock and its options go up or stay flat. Your odds of winning are two out of three.

Some investment gurus add two more stock behaviors for a total of five. The five are: the stock may stay flat, it may rise a little, it may rise a lot, it may drop a little, and it may drop a lot. Of these five conditions the naked put seller is a winner in four of the five scenarios. His investment value will only decline if the stock price drops a lot. This book will devote a good many pages and detailed trading illustrations on how to decrease or eliminate this loss factor.

BASICS

The trading system that will be the main focus of this book is based on the strategy of using the decaying characteristic of options to our advantage. Specifically it is the selling of calls and puts with the intention of letting the options expire worthless thereby allowing us to pocket the option premium obtained in the sale.

As already mentioned elsewhere in this book, statistically, and this is a well-known fact, 80% of all options expire worthless. Most options decay to the point of no value at expiration. If 80% of options lose value at expiration, it stands to reason that those who sold them made money! This is absolutely correct! Option sellers make money when the options they sold are not exercised by the option holder on or before the options expire. In other words the option seller makes money by patiently waiting for the option to lose its value due to time decay. Look at the Time Decay chart on Figure 1 and see how the passage of time erodes the value of options. The nearer they get to expiration the faster the decay.

As an investor you will place yourself in the shoes of the option seller and take advantage of this statistical fact. Based on this you may therefore conclude that most of the options you sell will decay and be winners at expiration and, the premiums you collected will accrue to you as profit. Now isn't that a beautiful statistic working in your favor? With enough care and attention and meticulously adhering to the system described in this book you will be enjoying consistent high returns on your capital.

This system's winning method is anchored on the strategy of selling put and call options. This involves the selling of OTM puts and calls. They can also be near expiration (three to six weeks away) or far out expiration (two to four months away). For those using near expiration options you will need to sell near-the-money strikes while those opting for far away expirations are able to sell far OTM strike prices. The advantage of one over the other becomes quite obvious when one looks at the premiums offered by the two types of options.

Short duration options, as you will see, pay out less in premiums while the farther durations are more generous in premiums. While shorter durations appear to provide less risk since the options will run for a shorter time, thus shortening your exposure time, they may be considered riskier for another reason. To get good premiums from shorter durations one must sell near-the-money strikes and this brings up the risk of getting ITM much easier than if one is into OTM strikes. Another attraction of selling shorter expiration options is that as the option nears maturity it losses value much faster as you can see from the steep downward curve shown in the Time Decay Chart below. But the other school of thought says that the longer you are out-of-the-money the longer you are exposed to the possibility that the option's strike price could eventually move into the money. It has not been firmly established which of the two schools of thought is the better strategy and the followers of each swear by their system. After weighing all the pros and cons of the two schools of thought it may seem that selling OTM strikes two to four months away is a more prudent strategy. Let us therefore, for the purpose of this instructional book, concentrate on selling OTM strikes at farther expiration dates.

FIGURE 1

Time Decay Chart

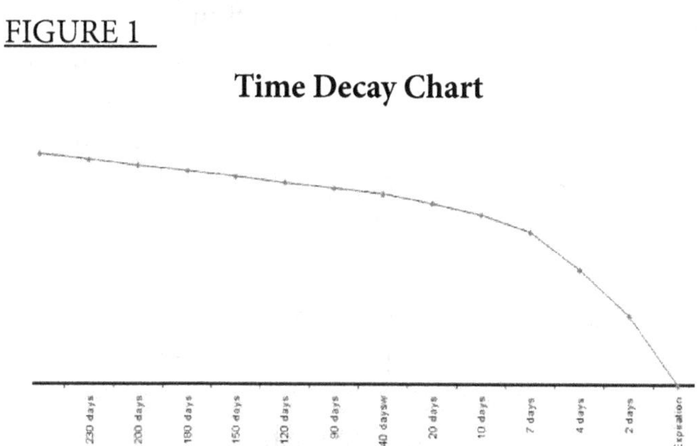

Next, we will create a ***modified credit ratio spread*** as a risk reduction strategy. Later on we will add one more risk reduction activity to complete this three pronged, nearly risk-free, trading system. I use the word ***modified*** because the credit ratio spread in our system will be created in a slightly different fashion from the normal credit ratio spread more commonly known to most option traders. In the normal ratio spread one sells a certain number of OTM options and simultaneously buys a lesser number of options at a near-the-money strike price. The ratio may be two to one or any other ratio that results in a credit in the trader's favor. To be sure you understand this, let's say some time in March you decide to do a credit ratio spread on XYZ CORP whose stock is at $50.50. You sell 10 June 42 puts at a premium of $2.30 for a total of $2,300 and at the same time buy 5 Jun 44 puts at $3.10 for a total of $1,550. The transaction results in a credit of $750 ($2,300 - $1,550) which is immediately added to the trader's account.

With the modified credit ratio spread as used in this book, instead of the simultaneous sell and buy of options we delay the buy side of the spread to a later date, if and when the market moves in the right direction, the direction favorable to us. Since we are trading both puts and calls – the market will always move in a favorable direction for one leg of the strangle giving us the opportunity to initiate the buy side of our credit spread. The advantage of this is that in the process of waiting for the market to move favorably to the point where we would form the long side of the credit spread, time will slowly eat away at the price of the proposed long option thereby allowing us to buy that option later at a reduced price.

Going back to the example above, you start by selling puts (assuming you are only doing puts and not getting into calls at this time) at a premium of $2.30 for a total of $2,300. At this point in time you do not initiate the buy side of puts but wait for the underlying security to rise in value before creating the long side of your position. Let's say XYZ Corp's stock did rise in value to say, $$52 per share after a few days or weeks. This is the time to create the long or buy side of the ratio spread. With XYZ at $52 per share the June 44 puts would now have a reduce premium of below the original $3.10. You could most likely buy 5 puts at around $2.80 or even lower. Now your ratio spread is yielding you $900 in profits instead of the original $750 if you had done the credit ratio spread at the onset of the trade.

Of course, the disadvantage is that if the market moves continuously in an adverse direction, downward, we may never be able to create the long side of the spread. But this also means that the opportunity for creating a modified credit spread will open on the other side of the strangle, i.e., if the put side loses the chance at a credit spread, the call side will likely be able to do so, and vice versa.

One more important feature of my option selling strategy which is not delved on deeply by other option selling books is the ability to roll out strike prices to farther dates. This is what I referred to earlier as the third step in the risk reducing ability of my trading system. I find this a very good protective course of action when our short position gets in a dangerous situation of possibly going ITM and could eventually be assigned. This is assuming that assignment is not a good choice for us in a particular situation and that we don't wish to own the underlying stock. Needless to say there may be situations where assignment may not be a bad thing. For instance, if we are short in puts and the underlying stock has undergone a long and steady decline in prices to the point where the stock is at a bargain price, it may not be a bad idea to allow our puts to be assigned and pick up the underlying stock at a give-away price.

Now that I have outlined the basic principles of my ***modified options selling investment system*** let me summarize the strategy before we proceed to the actual trading illustrations:

1. Sell call and put options on the same underlying stock. Choose strike prices and expiration periods that would provide premiums that are within your profit objectives and risk tolerance. Try as much as possible to go for strike prices farthest away from the underlying's current market price.

2. As we move toward expiration dates and the price of our underlying stock fluctuates up and down but never touches our strike prices, the put and call options will steadily lose value due to time decay to the point of being worthless at expiration. The premiums we collected from the sale of the options then become real profits.

3. But in the real world the price of the underlying stock seldom remains static within the trading range of our sold puts and calls. In the ensuing up down market fluctuations there will be opportunities for us to make adjustments in our positions so that we are constantly in profit all the time.

4. If the underlying stock price moves upward our put options lose value thereby giving us the chance for creating a modified ratio credit spread against the original puts we sold. This not only gives us partial protection on our put side in the event the market reverses (which happens quite frequently) but it also reduces our margin requirement on the original puts thereby releasing funds for new option positions. But our sold calls now rise in value. No problem! As long as the stock price does not touch our call strike price we do nothing on the call side. Depending on the extent and swiftness of the stock's increase in price, we may not need to make adjustments to our call options at this time.

5. In the event that the underlying stock price continues climbing to the point where it hits our call strike price we then roll out the option to a farther date and decrease the number of contracts. In the roll out process we always select options that will result in a break-even situation or very

minimal loss. This is demonstrated in the trading examples that follow later. Some traders will roll out to positions that will enable him to achieve a positive cash flow in the process instead of break-even or slight loss. I myself always try to aim at a positive cash situation in every roll-out. As the market rises we can do layering of positions by selling new put options either in the same underlying stock or with another security. In this way we are creating an inventory of positions with varied strike prices and varied expirations dates.

6. Should the market turn around and cause our underlying stock price to decline, the situation above reverses, with the call options losing value while the puts move up. A put roll out situation may arise if the downtrend continues long enough. In this event we roll out the puts by closing the ones that have gone at-the-money and roll out to farther out-of-the-money puts and farther dates. At the same time, depending on how much the market has declined, we may have a situation where we could create modified ratio credit spreads on the calls.

Now let's take a look at how the system works in its simplest form.

In April the NASDAQ 100 Trust Series (stock symbol QQQQ), an ETF stock, is trading at $34.05. Earlier on I mentioned that one could sell near-the-money or far out-of-the-money strikes, at near expiration or far expiration dates and the long term results would most likely be the same. I also mentioned that many option sellers consider the far expiration dates to be a more conservative play so in deference to the 'far expiration' followers, let's be more conservative and use longer expiration strikes in many of our trades in this book. In this scenario we decide to sell the June 29 puts at the price of $1.55.

Let me stop here for a moment to explain my choice of using puts in this illustration and in all the succeeding trading examples. I could have just as well used calls and it wouldn't have mattered much. For the rest of this e-book I will only be touching on one side of options and this will be puts. The reason I will not show the other side of the trading system is to make the instruction process as simple as possible for the learner to clearly grasp the subject. It is easier for the beginner to follow and learn only one side of my trading system than to take on the two sides simultaneously. For the beginner starting in the lucrative option selling business, it is good to start with puts. Later on as you gain experience and confidence in your trading activities you will want to do both calls and puts as this will increase your returns without adding capital. Just remember, exactly the same principles apply to calls as they do to puts. All the trading strategies using puts as illustrated in this e-book can be used in exactly the same fashion with calls. I strongly recommend that beginners start this trading system using puts and not get into the call side until you are extremely confident that you understand the process completely. I say this also because trading puts is safer than trading calls as there could be situations where there are risks in calls that do not apply to puts.

Going back to our illustration on QQQQ, selling the June 29 strike gave us a premium of $1.55 or $155 per contract which immediately gets credited into our broker account. We have just taken a $155 profit per contract up front and, unless the price of the underlying stock falls below $27.45 (our breakeven price), on or before the third Friday of June, the profit becomes a reality on that date. How did we arrive at our breakeven price of $27.45? It's the strike price of 29 less the premium of $1.55. Putting this in another perspective, if QQQQ's price drops to $29 on expiration day and the option holder calls the puts and assigns the stock to us, we will then have to buy the stock at $29. Assuming we are strictly option sellers not interested in owning stocks, we could turn around the next trading day and dispose of the stock at current market price. If it's still at $29, then that's what we sell it for. We broke even with the stock but made a profit of $1.55 from the put option we originally sold. But if on the following trading day after we were assigned the stock, it traded at $27.45 then we would have had to sell at that price and broken even on the entire transaction after factoring the $1.55 premium we got for the puts. If QQQQ trades at any price below $27.45 we would then start losing for every penny the price dropped below $27.45.

If we sold ten contracts our total cash intake would be $1,550 on this one transaction. Our capital? Let me stop here for a moment and talk about capital needs and returns on investment. In the options selling business you can either be secured or unsecured. Unsecured option selling is what we have been referring to as naked or uncovered selling. Selling secured puts means you have cash or other securities to finance the purchase of the stock if your sold puts expire in-the-money and you are assigned the stock. In our example of the XYZ stock you would need $29,000 in cash, or liquid securities deposited with your broker to cover the 10 contracts of June 29 puts. Actually your potential exposure is $29,000 less the $1,550 premium you collected or $27,450. This is what is termed as **cash secured put selling** which was discussed in Chapter 4. In a case where the option you sold expired worthless in June you would then pocket the $1,550 premium as profit or return on your investment. In this instance your ROI would be 5.6%, $1,550 as return on invested capital of $27,450. If you are able to do this several times in a year you could easily end up with an annual return in excess of 20%. If you were selling calls and you wanted to be 100% protected then you would actually need to own the underlying stock that you are selling calls against.

In naked option selling one sells options without the 100 percent cash security to cover the sold puts or one does not own stocks to cover the sold calls. Instead the option seller deposits a small cash amount and margins the balance. In our example the use of margin, which is offered by your options broker, allows you to put up only $3,310 to initiate the sale of 10 put contracts of XYZ Corp. That equates to a return of 46.8% in three months to expiration in June!

But not so fast! I don't want you to get blinded by this seemingly fantastic and easy way to make money! This is true only if you are a gambler and play this game like you're in a casino. If we are to use option selling as a safe investment vehicle then let's not be too adventurous and aggressive as using only $3,310 in support of a trade that yields a profit of $1,550. More on this when we get to the subject about Calculating Capital and Margin later in the book.

Continuing on with our first illustration on QQQQ, as mentioned earlier there are five ways a stock price may behave. The price may stay flat, it may rise a little, it may rise a lot, it may drop a little, or it may drop a lot. Of these five you are a winner in three scenarios and break-even in one. Your only problem is if the stock price drops a lot or drops continuously for a prolonged period of time. But as already mentioned previously this investment system has a safety feature that offers protection against serious damage. This safety feature is the ability of options to be rolled out. You will see this in more detail in the examples. I am surprised that in all the books I've read about option selling very few delve deeply in the loss protection benefits offered by the roll-out process. I am a believer in this process and my experience has proven that rolling out options that are getting at or in-the-money is a great way to decrease or totally eliminate losses.

CHAPTER SIX

Getting Started

Calculating Capital And Margin

In Chapter Four we discussed the strategy of selling puts using cash as security in order not to be in uncovered or naked status. In this chapter and for the following chapters we will be getting into the heat of what this book is all about and that is the strategy of selling naked options. Your first step is to establish a trading account with a securities broker who specializes in options trading. Let me say that again: a broker who specializes in options trading. You will definitely want to work with a specialist in options. Not all brokers are well versed in the complex world of options and if you should be unfortunate enough to land with a non-specialist you may have to put up more capital than is needed

Selling puts or calls without owning the underlying stock or having cash to cover the put side is in essence an uncovered or naked position. Brokers are required by securities regulations to demand from its clients a kind of security to cover naked positions. This is called maintenance margin. The maintenance margin required on each trade is equal to the underlying stock price times 20%, plus the premium received on the option sold, minus the amount by which the strike price is out-of-the-money, times 100 (contract lot). Did all this mumbo jumbo confuse you? Expressed in mathematical terms this is the way it looks:

Margin = (Stock price x 20%) + premium - amount by which option is OTM x 100.

The result of the above formula is the maintenance margin per contract. In deciding your initial capital commitment you must first comply with your stockbroker's minimum deposit requirement to open an account for options trading. This may be anywhere from $2,500 to as much as $10,000 or even higher depending on the broker. These funds will be used to secure the maintenance margins called for by securities regulations. This is why it is important to shop for a broker who allows trading in naked options without sticking you with a stiff capital requirement.

The above formula was used in calculating and arriving at the $3,310 maintenance margin on the ten contracts for QQQQ in our example.

$34.05 x .20 (20% of stock price) + 1.55 (option premium) – 5.05 (stock price less June 29 strike pr) x 100 = $331

The maintenance margin is $331 per contract and since you sold ten contracts, the total required margin is $3,310. You must have this amount in your broker's account in order to get your trade executed.

Now remember this margin deposit is not used in actual trade but is money parked in your brokerage account. For a broker to allow you to do this trade it will surely require you to deposit far more than just $3,310 in your account. If this was the only money you have with the broker you would be in a very tight position of being called for additional funds if your options moved in a negative direction. Because of this your broker will ask you for more funds up front than just $3,310. In this case a $5,000 deposit would most likely suffice. Each broker has his own way of calculating minimum deposits for clients and how much trading to allow the client. Since we want to be conservative investors we should work with a capital base that is sufficiently adequate to provide us with enough cushion to reduce trading risks. In the example given, if QQQQ stock were to decline to the price of our strike price of $29 at expiration date, and we did nothing to prevent possible assignment, the ten contracts could be exercised. We would then have to purchase 1,000 shares (10 contracts) of the underlying stock at $29 for a total of $29,000. As stated before, this may be a theoretical risk since there are alternatives to prevent exercise, but still the potential for this to happen exists. What if at expiration day you were on vacation and failed to notice that your put options had gone ITM? What if you were too sick on that day and couldn't take action to prevent assignment? What if there was a family emergency and you completely forgot to pay attention to your expiring options? What if...? What if...? What if...? Always keep enough funds in your broker account to meet this probability, if not entirely, at least enough to cover a large percentage of the total value of the potential assignment if it should happen. As a novice trader you should maintain your balance at a fairly high level and as you gain experience and confidence in options selling you can reduce the amount to a level you are comfortable with.

In the QQQQ example, assuming you are comfortable maintaining a balance of around 50% this amount would be somewhere around $14,500. This is what I would call my working capital and on which I calculate my yields, or rates of return. In the example, the rate of return at expiration, assuming your options expire worthless, would be 10.7%, $1,550 as a percentage of your working capital of $14,500.

Keep in mind the formula I listed above was the prevailing one at the time of writing this book. This may change from time to time as market conditions may dictate. It may also vary from broker to broker with some requiring stricter conditions while others are more lenient.

Selecting Stocks & Options

In my opinion any novice trader should not be selling options on non ETF stocks. I would limit this trading strategy to selling strictly ETF stocks (Exchange Traded Funds) or index options. I, even to this day and even with my many years of trading experience in option selling, continue to use mostly ETFs and indexes, and continue to stay away from company stocks. This is because I don't have the time nor the patience to study fundamentals, technicals and all the other mumbo jumbos of company stocks. Again, in the interest of reducing risks I find ETFs and indexes much less volatile than individual company stocks, thus lessening the risk factor. But if you must get into company stocks here are my guidelines in determining which stocks and options are best suited for the investment system of selling options whether puts or calls:

1. Select established profitable companies that have been in business for many years.

2. Look for stocks with a wide selection of option strike prices and select those whose options are actively traded. You can easily see which options are widely traded by just looking at the number of contracts which is reported in option chain tables under the column "open Interest"

3. Most importantly, avoid trading in stocks whose quarterly earnings reports are released within the same time span as the expiration date of the option you are planning to sell. A company's stock may undergo a dramatic price movement at the time the quarterly earnings report is released if the financials do not meet or exceed the expectations of Wall Street analysts. Example: It's February 14 and you decide to sell May options on Cisco Systems. The options you plan to sell expire on the third Friday of May. If Cisco's quarterly report is due for release between February 14th and the third Friday of May, its stock can undergo some wild gyrations prior to and after its financial report is released. It is therefore not a good idea to

trade Cisco options till after the report is released. Earnings release dates may be found on many web sites on the Internet.

4. Exchange Traded Funds or ETFs as well as indexes do not release quarterly earnings reports and are not closely followed by analysts. They are therefore free of the danger of gapping out due to price earnings reports. ETFs and indexes are excellent candidates for our investment system. If you don't already know, ETFs are stock mutual funds that are listed in the various exchanges and are traded just like regular stocks. Each ETF specializes in a specific market sector or index. Listed below are some of the more actively traded ETFs and indexes. More and more ETFs are being added constantly and there are now virtually dozens to choose from.

List Of Actively Traded ETFs:
QQQQ - NASDAQ 100 Trust Series
SMH - Merrill Lynch Semiconductor Index Trust
MDY - S&P Midcap 400 Index Trust
BBH - Biotech Holders Trust
IWM - Russell 2000 Index Trust
XLK - Technology Select
DIA - Dow Jones Industrial Index
SPY - S&P 500 Index
XLE - Energy Select Index
EEM - MSCI (Morgan Stanley) Emerging Markets Index
QLD – Pro Shares Ultra QQQ
XLF - Financial Select Sector SPDR Fund

List Of Actively Traded Indexes:
NDX - NASDAQ 100 index – European Style Expiration
OEX - S&P 100 index – American Style Expiration
XEO - S&P 100 index – European Style Expiration
SPX - S&P 500 index – European Style Expiration
DJX - Dow Jones index – European Style Expiration
RUT – Russell 2000 index – European Style Expiration

MID – S&P Midcap 400 Index – European Style Expiration
MNX – Mini NDX Index – European Style Expiration
XSP – Mini S&P Index (1/10th of full size contract) – European Style Expiration

Option picking services and newsletters

Using a stock picking service may be another alternative. These are firms or individuals who offer services selecting stocks for an investor according to the investor's investment goal. The Internet offers many such services for a variety of investment goals. For instance there are services that specialize in picking stocks for investors who like to invest in possible candidates for stock splits, stocks for investors who do short selling, stocks for environmentalists, penny stocks, medical research stocks, stocks that have fallen out of favor, high tech stocks, small cap stocks, upcoming IPO stocks, and so on and so forth. The list is nearly endless. What you want to look for are stocks, ETFs and indexes that are suitable for naked option selling. There are now various newsletters and web sites that offer option selling picks for option sellers. Most of them offer signals for credit spread option sellers but there are a few that offer signals for naked sellers. Using these services may be an excellent idea if you want assistance in determining when to do your trades. I myself subscribe to some just to see how they read the market. I use their signals as guides to complement my perception of the market. Not that I try to predict the market with their assistance, since I'm not a believer of basing my actions on market prediction, but it shows what option sellers are doing which gives me some idea of what I should do. Given that I don't do any fundamental, technical and market studies I kind of feel that the subscription fees I pay them are like professional consultation fees I pay for research services.

CHAPTER SEVEN

Actual trading illustrations

Now we come to the part of this book that is much awaited by the reader. In this chapter I will present trading illustrations on how to sell options in different market conditions using my three pronged trading system. Follow the examples slowly and analyze carefully the actions taken. I will be using the NASDAQ 100 Trust Series (symbol QQQQ) as the stock of choice because it meets all the criteria of the guidelines I listed for selecting stocks and options. My choice may be a biased one since the stock is an ETF and therefore less subject to wild fluctuations more common with ordinary stocks. You may choose any stock you feel comfortable with but do keep in mind that stocks meeting my guidelines have a big influencing factor on the outcome of your trades. I would also like to add that the quotes and premiums used in the illustrations were actual prices prevailing at the time I pulled them. Since writing this book I've received comments from some readers that today's prices are nowhere near as high as they were then. Yes I agree but those were the conditions at the time and those were the prices quoted then.

In order to measure our profitability at the end of the series of illustrations, we are going to assume a starting capital of $20,000 which will be deposited with our broker and which will be our working capital in the entire exercise.

ILLUSTRATION 1: Rising Market or Flat Market

Going back to the early part of this book I said that my option selling system is anchored on the strategy where we sell both call and put options on the same stock. The call and the put strikes need not necessarily be in the same future month. I also said that I would be showing trade examples in different market situations. In this first illustration you will learn to do trades when the market is rising and our trades will be initiated in response to the market's movement, not in anticipation of it. Let's get started.

Continuing on with the earlier example of selling QQQQ options, on April 3 the stock is trading at $34.05 when we decide to do our strangle. Figure 2 shows an option chain table from which we will select the options to trade. You should know by now that option sellers look at the 'bid' quotes in option tables while option buyers use the 'ask' quotes. Looking at the far out options (two to four months), we choose to sell the June 29 puts at a premium of $1.55. We could have chosen the June 28 or June 30 strike prices and the choice of which ones to sell is really dependent on how much premium one desires in conformity with his profit objectives and risk tolerance. We could have considered other farther months but upon looking at the list of future options we see that there are no July or August strikes. The next available options are in September and these are a bit too far. Although there are many option sellers that will go this distance and even longer. Next, we look at the other side of our strangle, the call side, and decide to do the June 41 strike price at a premium of $1.45. Without giving much thought to how the market will move we then proceed by selling the June 29 puts and the June 41 calls for a total premium intake of $3.00.

The June 29 strike price is about 15% below QQQQ's current stock value while the June 41 call is over 20% out giving us fairly wide latitude for the price of the underlying to move in either direction. This makes us comfortable in the thought that there is enough latitude to protect our positions if the market should swing in either direction and form a trend. This is not always the case as we shall see later.

NOTE: When this ebook was written there was then much volatility in the markets thus we were able to sell options with good premiums even with strike prices 15% to 20% away from the current underlying stock price. In a market with lower volatility strikes that are 8%-12% away from the current stock price may be good enough, although premiums will be lower. Keep in mind the farther the expiration of your option the greater should be the percentage of your strike price being away from the underlying price. For instance if you were looking at September puts you should be considering strikes that are over 20% away from the underlying's current price using the volatility levels prevailing when this ebook was written.

With $20,000 sitting in our broker account as our working capital we decide to sell 15 contracts of the June 29 puts giving us a cash intake of $2,325 and 15 contracts of the June 41 calls providing an inflow of $2,175 for an aggregate total cash intake of $4,500. This amount is immediately credited into our brokerage account. We have just taken $4,500 of profits up front and, if the price of the underlying stock remains on a trading range between $29 and $41 all the way till expiration date on the third Friday of June, the profit becomes a reality on that date.

FIGURE 2 (The quotes to the left of the strike months are calls and those on the right are puts)

Symbol(short)	Bid	Ask	Vol	OpInt	Delta	Symbol	Delta	OpInt	Vol	Ask	Bid	Symbol(short)
QQQ EP	0.7500	0.8000	1.51K	9.52K	26	MAY01 42.0000	-73	1.32K	10	8.6000	8.4000	QQQ QP
QQQ EQ	0.6000	0.6500	39	12.8K	23	MAY01 43.0000	-76	1.84K	18	9.4000	9.3000	QQQ QQ
QQQ ER	0.5000	0.5500	72	4.14K	20	MAY01 44.0000	-79	1.31K	58	10.3000	10.1000	QQQ QR
QQQ ES	0.4000	0.4500	4.26K	14.9K	18	MAY01 45.0000	-81	732	106	11.2000	11.1000	QQQ QS
QQQ ET	0.3000	0.3500	112	11.7K	15	MAY01 46.0000	-84	989	3	12.2000	12.0000	QQQ QT
QQQ EU	0.2500	0.3000	131	8.26K	13	MAY01 47.0000	-86	453	54	13.1000	12.9000	QQQ QU
QQQ EV	0.2000	0.2500	110	1.55K	11	MAY01 48.0000	-88	94	19	14.1000	13.9000	QQQ QV
QQQ EW	0.1500	0.2000	100	715	10	MAY01 49.0000	-89	159	59	15.0000	14.9000	QQQ QW
QQQ EX	0.1000	0.1500	1.13K	12.7K	8	MAY01 50.0000	-91	165	23	16.0000	15.8000	QQQ QX
QQQ EY	0.0500	0.1500	21	373	7	MAY01 51.0000	-92	112	83	17.0000	16.8000	QQQ QY
QQQ EZ	0.0500	0.1000	8	689	6	MAY01 52.0000	-93	38	1	18.0000	17.8000	QQQ QZ
QQQ EA	0.0500	0.1000	7	514	5	MAY01 53.0000	-94	28	10	19.0000	18.8000	QQQ QA
QQQ EB	0.0500	0.1000	10	431	4	MAY01 54.0000	-95		17	20.0000	19.8000	QQQ QB
QQQ EC	0.0500	0.0500	400	2.39K	4	MAY01 55.0000	-96	45	1	21.0000	20.8000	QQQ QC
QQQ ED	0.0500	0.0500	20	2.69K	3	MAY01 56.0000	-96	10	877	22.0000	21.8000	QQQ QD
QQQ EE	0.0500	0.0500	100	7.21K	2	MAY01 57.0000	-97		27	23.0000	22.8000	QQQ QE
QQQ EF	0.0500	0.0500	10	108	2	MAY01 58.0000	-97		575	24.0000	23.8000	QQQ QF
QQQ EG	0.0500	0.0500	4.53K	271	2	MAY01 59.0000	-98			25.0000	24.8000	QQQ QG
QQQ EH	0.0500	0.0500	10	3.94K	1	MAY01 60.0000	-98		6	26.0000	25.8000	QQQ QH
QUE EI	0.0500	0.0500	4	225	1	MAY01 61.0000	-98	4	140	27.0000	26.8000	QUE QI
QUE EJ	0.0500	0.0500	77	2.17K	1	MAY01 62.0000	-98			28.0000	27.8000	QUE QJ
QUE EK	0.0500	0.0500	66	159	1	MAY01 63.0000	-99			29.0000	28.8000	QUE QK
QUE EL	0.0500	0.0500	488	34	0	MAY01 64.0000	-99			30.0000	29.8000	QUE QL
QUE EM	0.0500	0.0500	3	120	0	MAY01 65.0000	-99	12	8	31.0000	30.8000	QUE QM
QUE EN	0.0500	0.0500	5	15	0	MAY01 66.0000	-99			32.0000	31.8000	QUE QN
QUE EO	0.0500	0.0500	275	5	0	MAY01 67.0000	-99			33.0000	32.8000	QUE QO
QUE EP	0.0500	0.0500	119	2.01K	0	MAY01 68.0000	-99			34.0000	33.8000	QUE QP
QUE EQ	0.0500	0.0500	18	7	0	MAY01 69.0000	-99			35.0000	34.8000	QUE QQ
QUE ER	0.0500	0.0500	23	5	0	MAY01 70.0000	-99			36.0000	35.8000	QUE QR
QUE ES	0.0500	0.0500	13	150	0	MAY01 71.0000	-99			37.0000	36.8000	QUE QS
QUE ET		0.0500		100	0	MAY01 72.0000	-99			38.0000	37.8000	QUE QT
QUE EU		0.0500	116	100	0	MAY01 73.0000	-100		116	39.0000	38.8000	QUE QU
YQQ EV		0.0500	1	100	0	MAY01 74.0000	-100			40.0000	39.8000	YQQ QV
YQQ EW		0.0500			0	MAY01 75.0000	-100			41.0000	40.8000	YQQ QW
YQQ EX		0.0500		90	0	MAY01 76.0000	-100			42.0000	41.8000	YQQ QX
YQQ EY		0.0500		90	0	MAY01 77.0000	-100			43.0000	42.8000	YQQ QY
YQQ EZ		0.0500		100	0	MAY01 78.0000	-100			44.0000	43.8000	YQQ QZ
YQQ EA		0.0500		100	0	MAY01 79.0000	-100			45.0000	44.8000	YQQ QA
YQQ EB		0.0500			0	MAY01 80.0000	-100	20	90	46.0000	45.8000	YQQ QB
QAV FZ	9.2000	9.3000			88	JUN01 26.0000	-12		400	0.9000	0.8500	QAV RZ
QAV FA	8.4000	8.4000			85	JUN01 27.0000	-14		23	1.1000	1.0500	QAV RA
QAV FB	7.6000	7.7000			82	JUN01 28.0000	-17			1.3500	1.3000	QAV RB
QAV FC	6.9000	7.0000			79	JUN01 29.0000	-21			1.6500	1.5500	QAV RC
QAV FD	6.2000	6.3000	161	708	75	JUN01 30.0000	-24	13.8K	1.53K	1.9500	1.9000	QAV RD
QAV FE	5.6000	5.7000	2	99	72	JUN01 31.0000	-28	2.79K	3	2.3500	2.2500	QAV RE
QAV FF	5.0000	5.0000	4	36	68	JUN01 32.0000	-31	2.59K	92	2.7000	2.6500	QAV RF
QAV FG	4.4000	4.5000	28	500	64	JUN01 33.0000	-35	1.78K	1.10K	3.1000	3.0000	QAV RG
QAV FH	3.9000	4.0000	115	139	61	JUN01 34.0000	-39	1.32K	426	3.6000	3.5000	QAV RH
QQQ FI	3.4000	3.5000	1.06K	2.58K	57	JUN01 35.0000	-42	3.77K	790	4.1000	4.0000	QQQ RI
QQQ FJ	3.0000	3.1000	224	2.34K	53	JUN01 36.0000	-46	4.03K	65	4.7000	4.6000	QQQ RJ
QQQ FK	2.6500	2.7000	323	503	50	JUN01 37.0000	-50	14.8K	68	5.3000	5.2000	QQQ RK
QQQ FL	2.3000	2.3500	6.23K	4.00K	46	JUN01 38.0000	-53	14.5K	896	6.0000	5.8000	QQQ RL
QQQ FM	2.0000	2.0000	420	6.85K	43	JUN01 39.0000	-56	7.18K	1.86K	6.7000	6.5000	QQQ RM
QQQ FN	1.7000	1.7500	3.12K	20.2K	40	JUN01 40.0000	-60	22.9K	2.31K	7.4000	7.2000	QQQ RN
QQQ FO	1.4500	1.5000	662	8.18K	37	JUN01 41.0000	-63	9.03K	1.81K	8.1000	8.0000	QQQ RO
QQQ FP	1.2500	1.3000	239	16.3K	34	JUN01 42.0000	-66	9.45K	84	8.9000	8.8000	QQQ RP
QQQ FQ	1.0500	1.1000	161	4.52K	31	JUN01 43.0000	-69	14.4K	51	9.8000	9.6000	QQQ RQ
QQQ FR	0.9000	0.9500	1.45K	15.0K	28	JUN01 44.0000	-71	8.13K	12	10.6000	10.4000	QQQ RR
QQQ FS	0.7500	0.8000	795	27.4K	26	JUN01 45.0000	-74	6.83K	42	11.5000	11.3000	QQQ RS
QQQ FT	0.6500	0.7000	211	1.54K	23	JUN01 46.0000	-76	1.46K	6	12.4000	12.2000	QQQ RT
QQQ FU	0.5500	0.6000	205	3.43K	21	JUN01 47.0000	-78	4.02K	16	13.3000	13.1000	QQQ RU
QQQ FV	0.4500	0.5000	64	6.07K	19	JUN01 48.0000	-80	1.47K	2	14.2000	14.0000	QQQ RV
QQQ FW	0.3500	0.4000	36	3.43K	17	JUN01 49.0000	-82	1.73K	59	15.2000	15.0000	QQQ RW
QQQ FX	0.3000	0.3500	2.35K	31.9K	16	JUN01 50.0000	-84	19.7K	78	16.1000	15.9000	QQQ RX
QQQ FY	0.2500	0.3000	83	2.78K	14	JUN01 51.0000	-85	669	7	17.1000	16.9000	QQQ RY
QQQ FZ	0.2000	0.2500	166	5.04K	13	JUN01 52.0000	-87	1.18K	3	18.0000	17.8000	QQQ RZ
QQQ FA	0.1500	0.2500	72	3.13K	11	JUN01 53.0000	-88	900	10	19.0000	18.8000	QQQ RA
QQQ FB	0.1500	0.2000	2	3.40K	10	JUN01 54.0000	-89	2.84K	83	20.0000	19.8000	QQQ RB
QQQ FC	0.1500	0.2000	202	25.9K	9	JUN01 55.0000	-90	2.04K	66	21.0000	20.8000	QQQ RC
QQQ FD	0.1000	0.1500	237	12.5K	8	JUN01 56.0000	-91	6.89K	5	22.0000	21.8000	QQQ RD
QQQ FE	0.0500	0.1000	80	3.84K	7	JUN01 57.0000	-92	10.7K	1	23.0000	22.8000	QQQ RE

From here on forward the illustrations that follow will show only the put side of trading in order not to complicate the system for the novice who is following the trades and carefully learning the process. The step by step instructions and the resultant transactions will involve numerous operations. Adding the call side to the whole equation may only serve to totally confuse the learner. The transactions that will be demonstrated on the put side alone are going to be quite a number. Suffice it to say, all the principles applied in trading puts work the same way with calls, only in reverse. It is my hope that the reader will first start trading puts for a while and as he gains more knowledge and experience he can see how the same actions apply to calls and he can then start trading the call side as well. One thing to remember is that good options brokers will require maintenance margins only on one side of the trading position, not on both sides. In the example above the maintenance margin will be computed only on the put side since this is the side that requires a higher margin. If you have a broker that tells you to margin both sides of the trade, it's time to find another broker who knows that the client can't be at risk on both sides.

Okay, we've just done our first trades. We now sit back and wait for the calls and puts to decay as they move toward expiration. As stated earlier we will monitor only the put side and show illustrations about trading puts only. Let's now disregard trades on the call side.

As time moves on we occasionally monitor the behavior of QQQQ stock to ensure that it does not move down far enough to hit our strike price of 29. It may even move farther down to our break-even point of $27.45 before we decide to take action. What happens if the stock does go down to these levels? We could be assigned the stock, where the option holder may exercise the option in which case we would have to buy the underlying stock at the price of $29. In some cases the option seller (we) may prefer to be assigned the stock but for purposes of this exercise let's assume that we elect not to do so unless and until we reach a point where we run out of alternatives.

Let me pause here a minute and let me repeat what I have already said about assignments. Since our put strike price is $29 this means that if/when the underlying's price drops to $29 or below, the option may be exercised and we would have to buy the stock at $29 per share regardless of how low the price has dropped. As long as the price does not drop below $27.45 we still stand to gain if we are assigned at any price between $29 and $27.45. How? Let's say the stock drops down to $28.00, the option is exercised and we are assigned the stock. This means we have to buy the stock at $29 which is the strike price at which we sold the put option. Having now the stock in hand we can then turn around and sell it at the market price of $28.00. While we seem to have lost $1.00 in this transaction we actually made a $0.55 profit since we originally sold the option at $1.55. Of course there are fees and charges associated in the assignment process so the net profit will actually be a little less than $0.55. In real life it is seldom that ITM puts are exercised by the holder. The more common thing to do is for the put holder to just sell his puts that are now ITM which by then are probably quoted at much more than the $1.55 that he paid for them when we sold them. Assignment would happen if the option holder actually owned the stock and is now more interested in disposing of the underlying shares. If he were just a speculator he would have bought the puts from us strictly with the intention of selling them when the underlying's price dropped and the puts rose in value.

In my trading experience I seldom ever wait for the underlying's price to drop below my strike price before initiating corrective measures. I immediately go into action using the powerful protective feature of rolling out my naked options. This is the key element in my option selling system and is a potent safety feature that prevents or defers the possibility of assignment. In the roll out process, I not only go to longer expirations but I also decrease the number of contracts in play. This will be discussed in more detail later and there will be many trading illustrations involving the use of the roll-out method. For right now let's look at the situation when the stock price is in an uptrend to demonstrate the trades done in this type of market direction.

On April 10 we note the market has become active and QQQQ has gone up to $39.80, over $5 higher than when we entered our first trade. This creates an opportunity to initiate a ratio spread on our puts. Looking at the table on Figure 3 we see that the price of our June 29 put has decayed nicely down to the level of $0.65-$0.70. Further, we see that we can now buy the long side of our ratio spread at very attractive prices. We decide to buy 7 contracts of the June 33 puts at $1.45. I like to do ratios of two to one on my ratio spreads although you may use any ratio you wish, again depending on your trading style and profit objectives. We now have 7 long put contracts offering protection to our 15 short put contracts. What this means is that should the market reverse and start dropping the long positions would offer a good degree of protection against losses on the shorts. Remember what I said that I use a modified type of ratio credit spread? I call it modified because I wait to form the long side of the spread at a later date instead of at the same time that I sold the puts. Let me explain why I like initiating the long side at a later date when the market has moved favorably in my direction.

If in our initial trade on April 3rd we had coupled the naked puts to a credit ratio spread, we would have had to buy the 7 contracts of June 33 puts at $3.10 costing $2,170 resulting in a net credit in our account of only $155 ($2,325 – 2,170). If we wanted a better cash intake we would have had to buy puts at a strike price nearer our short option of June 29, probably the June 31 strike which then was priced at $2.35. This would have still yielded a net of only $680 for the same seven contracts. Not only is the yield smaller but the distance between the two strikes, the short June 29 and the long June 31, is now narrower. One thing to remember in ratio credit spreads is that the farther apart the strike prices are, the greater the ability of the long side protecting the short side. Put differently, the farther apart the strikes, the greater the safety factor.

FIGURE 3 (The quotes to the left of the strike months are calls and those on the right are puts)

Symbol(short)	Bid	Ask	Vol	Opint	Delta	Symbol	Delta	Opint	Vol	Ask	Bid	Symbol(short)
QQQ EN	3.20	3.40	15.6K	30.1K	53	MAY01 40.00	-46	9.04K	2.41K	3.40	3.20	QQQ QN
QQQ EO	2.75	2.85	1.16K	10.3K	48	MAY01 41.00	-51	4.05K	221	3.90	3.80	QQQ QO
QQQ EP	2.35	2.45	3.55K	10.7K	44	MAY01 42.00	-55	1.43K	384	4.50	4.30	QQQ QP
QQQ EQ	2.00	2.10	1.12K	21.5K	40	MAY01 43.00	-60	1.84K	26	5.10	5.00	QQQ QQ
QQQ ER	1.65	1.75	632	4.53K	35	MAY01 44.00	-64	1.26K	23	5.80	5.70	QQQ QR
QQQ ES	1.40	1.45	2.89K	20.5K	32	MAY01 45.00	-68	747	116	6.60	6.40	QQQ QS
QQQ ET	1.15	1.25	3.15K	20.7K	28	MAY01 46.00	-71	995	20	7.30	7.10	QQQ QT
QQQ EU	0.95	1.00	539	8.37K	25	MAY01 47.00	-74	451	16	8.10	7.90	QQQ QU
QQQ EV	0.80	0.85	90	1.90K	22	MAY01 48.00	-77	104	231	8.90	8.70	QQQ QV
QQQ EW	0.65	0.70	658	1.16K	19	MAY01 49.00	-80	161	109	9.80	9.60	QQQ QW
QQQ EX	0.50	0.60	1.21K	12.6K	17	MAY01 50.00	-83	213	59	10.70	10.50	QQQ QX
QQQ EY	0.45	0.50	21	358	14	MAY01 51.00	-85	98	9	11.60	11.40	QQQ QY
QQQ EZ	0.35	0.40	1	687	12	MAY01 52.00	-87	29	125	12.50	12.30	QQQ QZ
QQQ EA	0.25	0.35	23	514	11	MAY01 53.00	-89	26	23	13.50	13.30	QQQ QA
QQQ EB	0.20	0.25	15	449	9	MAY01 54.00	-90	17	151	14.40	14.20	QQQ QB
QQQ EC	0.15	0.20	160	2.86K	8	MAY01 55.00	-92	45	149	15.40	15.20	QQQ QC
QQQ ED	0.10	0.20	3.21K	2.69K	6	MAY01 56.00	-93	9	3.33K	16.40	16.10	QQQ QD
QQQ EE	0.10	0.15	13	7.21K	5	MAY01 57.00	-94		2.11K	17.30	17.10	QQQ QE
QQQ EF	0.10	0.10	113	108	5	MAY01 58.00	-95		110	18.30	18.10	QQQ QF
QQQ EG	0.05	0.10	2	271	4	MAY01 59.00	-95			19.30	19.10	QQQ QG
QQQ EH	0.05	0.10	15	4.05K	3	MAY01 60.00	-96	16	1.31K	20.30	20.10	QQQ QH
QUE EI	0.05	0.05	4	225	3	MAY01 61.00	-97	4	8	21.30	21.10	QUE QI
QUE EJ	0.05	0.05	4	2.17K	2	MAY01 62.00	-97			22.30	22.10	QUE QJ
QUE EK	0.05	0.05	6	159	2	MAY01 63.00	-98			23.30	23.10	QUE QK
QUE EL	0.05	0.05	3.33K	34	1	MAY01 64.00	-98			24.30	24.10	QUE QL
QUE EM	0.05	0.05	206	120	1	MAY01 65.00	-98	12	7	25.30	25.10	QUE QM
QUE EN	0.05	0.05	357	15	1	MAY01 66.00	-98			26.30	26.10	QUE QN
QUE EO	0.05	0.05		5	1	MAY01 67.00	-99			27.30	27.10	QUE QO
QUE EP	0.05	0.05	26	2.01K	0	MAY01 68.00	-99			28.30	28.10	QUE QP
QUE EQ	0.05	0.05		7	0	MAY01 69.00	-99			29.30	29.10	QUE QQ
QUE ER	0.05	0.05	5	5	0	MAY01 70.00	-99			30.30	30.10	QUE QR
QUE ES	0.05	0.05	2	150	0	MAY01 71.00	-99			31.30	31.10	QUE QS
QUE ET	0.05	0.05		100	0	MAY01 72.00	-99			32.30	32.10	QUE QT
QUE EU	0.05	0.05		100	0	MAY01 73.00	-99			33.30	33.10	QUE QU
YQQ EV	0.55	0.05		100	0	MAY01 74.00	-99			34.30	34.10	YQQ QV
YQQ EW		0.05			0	MAY01 75.00	-99			35.30	35.10	YQQ QW
YQQ EX	0.05	0.05		90	0	MAY01 76.00	-99			36.30	36.10	YQQ QX
YQQ EY	0.05	0.05		90	0	MAY01 77.00	-100			37.30	37.10	YQQ QY
YQQ EZ	0.05	0.05		100	0	MAY01 78.00	-100			38.30	38.10	YQQ QZ
YQQ EA	0.05	0.05		100	0	MAY01 79.00	-100			39.30	39.10	YQQ QA
YQQ EB		0.05			0	MAY01 80.00	-100	20		40.30	40.10	YQQ QB
QAV FY	15.20	15.40	25	27	96	JUN01 25.00	-3	992	1.18K	0.30	0.25	QAV RY
QAV FZ	14.30	14.40			95	JUN01 26.00	-4	2.22K	1	0.35	0.30	QAV RZ
QAV FA	13.30	13.50			93	JUN01 27.00	-6	1.40K	31	0.45	0.40	QAV RA
QAV FB	12.50	12.60			92	JUN01 28.00	-8	23	22	0.55	0.50	QAV RB
QAV FC	11.60	11.70	10		90	JUN01 29.00	-10	2	1	0.70	0.65	QAV RC
QAV FD	10.70	10.90	151	733	87	JUN01 30.00	-12	14.5K	2.18K	0.85	0.75	QAV RD
QAV FE	9.90	10.10	2	98	85	JUN01 31.00	-15	2.76K	1	1.00	0.95	QAV RE
QAV FF	9.10	9.30	3	41	82	JUN01 32.00	-17	3.84K	120	1.20	1.15	QAV RF
QAV FG	8.40	8.60	2	731	79	JUN01 33.00	-20	2.69K	266	1.45	1.40	QAV RG
QAV FH	7.60	7.80	13	202	76	JUN01 34.00	-23	2.02K	797	1.65	1.60	QAV RH
QQQ FI	6.90	7.10	262	3.26K	73	JUN01 35.00	-27	6.08K	1.07K	2.00	1.90	QQQ RI
QQQ FJ	6.30	6.50	308	3.03K	69	JUN01 36.00	-30	10.7K	168	2.35	2.25	QQQ RJ
QQQ FK	5.70	5.80	317	5.26K	66	JUN01 37.00	-34	18.5K	1.17K	2.65	2.65	QQQ RK
QQQ FL	5.10	5.20	541	10.1K	62	JUN01 38.00	-37	16.5K	2.01K	3.10	3.00	QQQ RL
QQQ FM	4.50	4.70	195	7.31K	59	JUN01 39.00	-41	7.02K	554	3.60	3.50	QQQ RM
QQQ FN	4.00	4.20	1.92K	20.2K	55	JUN01 40.00	-44	22.2K	1.92K	4.10	3.90	QQQ RN
QQQ FO	3.60	3.70	752	8.78K	52	JUN01 41.00	-48	8.09K	56	4.60	4.50	QQQ RO
QQQ FP	3.10	3.20	306	16.4K	48	JUN01 42.00	-51	9.42K	28	5.10	5.00	QQQ RP
QQQ FQ	2.80	2.85	225	5.55K	45	JUN01 43.00	-54	14.4K	81	5.70	5.60	QQQ RQ
QQQ FR	2.45	2.50	165	14.1K	42	JUN01 44.00	-58	8.11K	5	6.50	6.30	QQQ RR
QQQ FS	2.10	2.20	8.92K	27.4K	39	JUN01 45.00	-61	6.89K	249	7.10	7.00	QQQ RS
QQQ FT	1.85	1.90	213	1.52K	36	JUN01 46.00	-64	1.45K	20	7.90	7.70	QQQ RT
QQQ FU	1.60	1.70	1.20K	3.58K	33	JUN01 47.00	-67	4.01K	1	8.60	8.40	QQQ RU
QQQ FV	1.40	1.45	132	6.16K	30	JUN01 48.00	-69	1.44K	231	9.40	9.20	QQQ RV
QQQ FW	1.15	1.25	109	3.41K	28	JUN01 49.00	-72	1.73K	1	10.20	10.00	QQQ RW
QQQ FX	1.00	1.10	1.81K	31.9K	25	JUN01 50.00	-74	19.6K	23	11.00	10.90	QQQ RX
QQQ FY	0.85	0.95	15	2.86K	23	JUN01 51.00	-76	665	9	11.90	11.70	QQQ RY
QQQ FZ	0.75	0.80	125	5.10K	21	JUN01 52.00	-78	1.30K	7	12.80	12.60	QQQ RZ
QQQ FA	0.60	0.70	23	3.11K	19	JUN01 53.00	-80	900	10	13.70	13.50	QQQ RA
QQQ FB	0.55	0.60	10	3.40K	17	JUN01 54.00	-82	2.79K	1	14.60	14.40	QQQ RB

After forming the ratio spread, the margin requirement on the put side has been decreased because the 7 long puts we purchased now serve to cover 7 short puts leaving only 8 puts naked or uncovered. The funds released from margin now becomes available to margin new positions if we choose to do so. Let's assume at this point we decide not to open any new positions as it is too soon after our initial trade of April 3rd.

Here is what our broker account looks like after doing the ratio spread:

April 3: Initial funds deposited with broker	$20,000
April 3: Sold 15 contracts June 29 puts @ $1.55	2,325
April 10: Bought 7 contracts June 33 puts @ 1.45	- 1,015
Cash balance in broker account	21,310

Actually the money in our account is more than what is showing since we have not added in the premium received from the sale of calls. Let's just leave it as it is for the time being and assume we are not trading calls just yet as you learn the mechanics of this trading system.

Note that I have not included broker's fees and other charges in my numbers as these are very much dependent on your broker's fees and exchange fees. Needless to say, the charges do not really amount to big enough numbers to have a great deal of influence on the over-all returns. If you were a day trader doing multiple trades in a day they do count and should certainly be factored in your costs. But we are not day traders and our trades are few enough that fees are negligible.

As we march on to the expiration date in June, we see that QQQ's stock price has continued an upward trend reaching a high of $48.40. It then began to decline so that on April 23rd when it is at $45.15 we decide to do another sale of puts. Looking at the option table for this date we find that the September 35 strike offers a fairly attractive premium of $2.00. There are still no July and August strikes so we had to go with September since the June 35 strike did not offer a good premium.

We sell 8 September 35 puts and collect $1,600 in the process. Our total naked holdings now consist of 8 naked June 29 puts (the remaining seven are covered by our June 33 long puts) and 8 September 35s totaling sixteen naked puts. My reason for mentioning only the naked puts is because these are the ones that require maintenance margins. The short puts that are covered by the long puts don't need margin.

The market once again turns around and goes upward, continuing the trend until QQQQ reaches a price of $48.09 on May 18th. At this point we again decide to do a ratio credit spread on our last sale of September 35 puts. This time we choose to buy 4 Sept 40 puts at $1.90 costing us a total of $760.

Here is what our account looks like after the transaction:

April 3: Initial funds deposited with broker	$20,000
April 3: Sold 15 contracts June 29 puts @ $1.55	2,325
April 10: Bought 7 contracts June 33 puts @ $1.45	- 1,015
April 23: Sold 8 Sept 35 puts @ $2.00	1,600
May 18: Bought 4 Sept 40 puts @ $1.90	- 760
Cash balance in broker account	22,150

Then on May 30, after the market danced up and down without a clear direction we decided to sell more puts to increase our number of open positions following a layering strategy. Layering is just another term for diversifying. What we are doing is diversifying into various positions at different strike prices and expirations. In this illustration I've been using only the QQQQ security but you may actually use a combination of different securities for your diversified portfolio. In fact a well layered portfolio should consist of different securities for better diversification.

With the underlying stock at a price of $44.27 on May 30th we sell ten Sept 38 puts at a premium of $2.00 taking in a total of $2,000 on this transaction. Keep in mind the additional maintenance margin requirements are being covered by the cash inflows not only from the puts but also from the sales of call options that are also being done on the other side. Although I am not listing the call transactions, these are happening in the same way that the puts are. By not listing the call transactions I'm keeping my promise to not muddle the reader's mind with so much clutter of so many transactions. But do keep in mind that trading in call options continues to go on.

Nothing else is done on the put side until mid June. On this date the June 29 and June 33 puts expired and no action is required of us. On the following Monday after expiration we set out to sell new options to replace the expired ones and continue layering our various open positions. This time with the stock at $42.14, we sell ten of the Sept 37 puts at $1.90, taking a total intake of $1,900.

Here is our account position on June 18:

April 3:	Initial funds deposited with broker	$20,000
April 3:	Sold 15 contracts June 29 puts @ $1.55(expired)	2,325
April 10:	Bought 7 contracts June 33 puts @ 1.45(expired)	- 1,015
April 23:	Sold 8 Sept 35 puts @ $2.00	1,600
May 18:	Bought 4 Sept 40 puts @ $1.90	- 760
May 30:	Sell 10 Sept 38 puts @ $2.00	2,000
June 18:	Sell 10 Sept 37 puts @ $1.90	1,900
	Cash balance in broker account	26,050

On June 29 QQQQ goes up to a price of $46.00. We decide to create a ratio spread on our Sept 37 puts by buying 5 Sep 42 puts at $1.85 for a total cost of $925. For one reason or another no further trades are done during the following month of July. On August 1st, with QQQQ at $43.01 we sell eight Sep 39 puts at $1.05 and collect $840.

Our account balance on August 1st:

April 3:	Initial funds deposited with broker	$20,000
April 3:	Sold 15 contracts June 29 puts @ $1.55 (expired)	2,325
April 10:	Bought 7 contracts June 33 puts @ 1.45 (expired)	- 1,015
April 23:	Sold 8 Sept 35 puts @ $2.00	1,600
May 18:	Bought 4 Sept 40 puts @ $1.90	- 760
May 30:	Sell 10 Sept 38 puts @ $2.00	2,000
June 18:	Sell 10 Sept 37 puts @ $1.90	1,900
June 29:	Bought 5 Sept 42 puts @ $1.85	- 925
Aug 1:	Sold 8 Sep 39 puts @ $1.05	840
	Cash balance in broker account	25,965

This ends our illustration on how to trade options in a market that is on a trading pattern (no direction) as well as in a rising market. The next illustration will demonstrate trades in a dropping market and will show how to use the rolling out process to protect positions that may be in danger of going in-the-money.

ILLUSTRATION 2: Down Market

Continuing on with our trades of the previous illustration, on August 10 the stock market changes direction and QQQQ stock declines to a price of $39.65. This brings it close to our Sept 39 puts that we just recently sold on August 1. It makes us nervous that the stock's price is so close to our strike price with still a month left to expiration. We are afraid that if the stock continues downward it might eventually decline to the level of our 39 strike and may even go in-the-money. This would leave us exposed to the possibility of assignment with expiration not so far away. We decide to do a roll-out and place ourselves out of harm's way. Here's how a roll out is done. We buy back the Sept 39 puts which are now priced higher at $2.00 and sell new puts in its place with a far out expiration so that we can recover the buy-back money. Furthermore, in the roll out process we wish to reduce our risk exposure by selling fewer contracts of the far out puts. This is what we do:

Buy back the 8 contracts of Sept 39 puts at $2.00 and sell 3 contracts of the Jan 2003 puts with strike price of 35 at a premium of $4.50. The new puts are fifteen months away and even if these go in-the-money it is very remote that they would be exercised with expiration so far away. Even if they were exercised, we are only exposed to 3 contracts instead of the original 8 contracts. A much more palatable situation.

Here is what our account balance looks like:

April 3:	Initial funds deposited with broker	$20,000
April 3:	Sold 15 contracts June 29 puts @ $1.55 (expired)	2,325
April 10:	Bought 7 contracts June 33 puts @ 1.45 (expired)	- 1,015
April 23:	Sold 8 Sept 35 puts @ $2.00	1,600
May 18:	Bought 4 Sept 40 puts @ $1.90	- 760
May 30:	Sell 10 Sept 38 puts @ $2.00	2,000
Jun 18:	Sell 10 Sept 37 puts @ $1.90	1,900
Jun 29:	Bought 5 Sept 42 puts @ $1.85	- 925
Aug 1:	Sold 8 Sep 39 puts @ $1.05	840
Aug 10:	Bought to close 8 contracts of Sept 39 @ $2.00	-1,600
Aug 10	Sold to 3 contracts of Jan 35 puts (2003) @ $4.50	1,350
	Cash balance in broker account	25,715

This latest trade produced a negative effect on our cash balance but the obvious benefit is that it removed, at least for the time being, an immediate potential threat.

The market continued on a steady decline and on August 17 QQQQ stood at a low price of $37.76. This comes close to our Sept 37 puts (sold on June 18) and again we decide not to wait any longer and do another roll-out. We do the following:

Buy back to close 10 Sep 37 puts @ 1.70 (sold on June 18)	- $1,700
Sell 6 contracts of Jan 30 puts, 2003	1,800

Once again we rolled out 10 contracts into a reduced quantity of 6 contracts and put ourselves out of harm's way for a long time, that is, until the year 2003.

As we make an inventory of our positions on August 17 we note that our Sept 38 puts (sold on May 30) are now close to the current market price of the underlying. We get nervous and decide to roll this out as well and do the following:

Buy back to close the10 Sept 38 puts @ 2.20	- 2,200
Sell to open 6 contracts of Jan 30 puts (2004) @ $4.00	2,400

Here is what our account balance looks like:

April 3:	Initial funds deposited with broker	$20,000
April 3:	Sold 15 contracts June 29 puts @ $1.55 (expired)	2,325
April 10:	Bought 7 contracts June 33 puts @ 1.45 (expired)	- 1,015
April 23:	Sold 8 Sept 35 puts @ $2.00	1,600
May 18:	Bought 4 Sept 40 puts @ $1.90	- 760
May 30:	Sell 10 Sept 38 puts @ $2.00	2,000
Jun 18:	Sell 10 Sept 37 puts @ $1.90	1,900
Jun 29:	Bought 5 Sept 42 puts @ $1.85	- 925

Aug 1:	Sold 8 Sep 39 puts @ $1.05	840
Aug 10:	Bought to close 8 contracts of Sept 39 @ $2.00	-1,600
Aug 10	Sold to 3 contracts of Jan 35 puts (2003) @ $4.50	1,350
Aug 17:	Bought to close 10 Sept 37s @ $1.70 (sold on June 18)	-1,700
Aug 17:	Sold 6 Jan 30 puts (2003) @ $3.00	1,800
Aug 17:	Bought 10 Sept 38s @ $2.20	-2.200
Aug 17:	Sold 6 Jan 30 puts (2004) @ $4.00	2,400
	Cash balance in broker account	26,015

On August 30th we again find ourselves in a situation to need another roll-out when QQQQ goes farther down to $36.17. Our Sept 35 puts (sold on April 23) are now close to the market price and seeing the continuing declining trend of the market we decide not to wait and we take immediate action. Now here is a situation that may not call for a roll out. The Sept 35 puts have now decayed to a price of only $1.00 which means that buying back the 8 contracts would only put us out $800. Closing out the position frees us to write a new set of puts. We therefore decide to just close them out. But instead of selling new puts we are concerned about the continuing downtrend and decide to do nothing and wait a while before replacing the closed puts.

Here is what our account balance looks like:

April 3:	Initial funds deposited with broker	$20,000
April 3:	Sold 15 contracts June 29 puts @ $1.55	2,325
April 10:	Bought 7 contracts June 33 puts @ 1.45	- 1,015
April 23:	Sold 8 Sept 35 puts @ $2.00	1,600
May 18:	Bought 4 Sept 40 puts @ $1.90	- 760
May 30:	Sell 10 Sept 38 puts @ $2.00	2,000
Jun 18:	Sell 10 Sept 37 puts @ $1.90	1,900
Jun 29:	Bought 5 Sept 42 puts @ $1.85	- 925
Aug 1:	Sold 8 Sep 39 puts @ $1.05	840
Aug 10:	Bought to close 8 contracts of Sept 39 @ $2.00	-1,600

Aug 10:	Sold to 3 contracts of Jan 35 puts (2003) @ $4.50	1,350
Aug 17:	Bought to close 10 Sept 37s @ $1.70 (sold on June 18)	-1,700
Aug 17:	Sold 6 Jan 30 puts (2003) @ $3.00	1,800
Aug 17:	Bought 10 Sept 38s @ $2.20	-2.200
Aug 17:	Sold 6 Jan 30 puts (2004) @ $4.00	2,400
Aug 30:	Bought to close 8 Sept 30 puts (sold on April 23) @ $1.00	-800
	Cash balance in broker account	25,215

September comes around and we find there is no let up in the market's downward trend. But now this fact works in our favor. The long positions of the ratio credit spreads that we created in the early part of our trading activities have gained much value. With QQQQ trading at $33.70 on September 7 and expiration dates not too far away, we decide to close the long puts and take profits. At this time the market has had a long downward run and it just might be possible that it may now be at its end. Following my philosophy of trading in response to the market this tells me that it would not be a bad idea to sell new put positions at this low point in the market. Here is what we do:

Sell to close the 4 long Sept 40 puts @ $6.30 and the 5 long Sept 42 puts @ $8.20 giving us a total cash inflow of $6,620. At the same time we sell ten naked Dec 30 puts @ $1.80 for another intake of $1,799.

Here is what our account balance looks like:

April 3:	Initial funds deposited with broker	$20,000
April 3:	Sold 15 contracts June 29 puts @ $1.55	2,325
April 10:	Bought 7 contracts June 33 puts @ 1.45	- 1,015
April 23:	Sold 8 Sept 35 puts @ $2.00	1,600
May 18:	Bought 4 Sept 40 puts @ $1.90	- 760
May 30:	Sell 10 Sept 38 puts @ $2.00	2,000

Jun 18:	Sell 10 Sept 37 puts @ $1.90	1,900
Jun 29:	Bought 5 Sept 42 puts @ $1.85	- 925
Aug 1:	Sold 8 Sep 39 puts @ $1.05	840
Aug 10:	Bought to close 8 contracts of Sept 39 @ $2.00	-1,600
Aug 10:	Sold to 3 contracts of Jan 35 puts (2003) @ $4.50	1,350
Aug 17:	Bought to close 10 Sept 37s @ $1.70 (sold on June 18)	-1,700
Aug 17:	Sold 6 Jan 30 puts (2003) @ $3.00	1,800
Aug 17:	Bought 10 Sept 38s @ $2.20	-2.200
Aug 17:	Sold 6 Jan 30 puts (2004) @ $4.00	2,400
Aug 30:	Bought to close 8 Sept 30 puts (sold on April 23) @ $1.00	-800
Sept 7:	Sold to close 4 Sept 40 puts (bought on May 18) @ 6.30	2,520
Sept 7:	Sold to close 5 Sept 42 puts (bought on June 29) @ 8.20	4,100
Sept 7:	Sold 10 Dec 30 puts @ 1.80	1,800
	Cash balance in broker account	33,635

Having reached this point in our trading examples I'm sure you have now gotten a good idea of what selling options is all about. The prices I've used for the illustrations were taken from actual prices of QQQQ options in the year 2001. I chose to use the date range of April to September because it enabled me to illustrate the trades required when the market was up-trending (April-May), then got stuck in a trading pattern with no discernible direction (June to early-August), and finally went on a decline (mid-August to September). As you can see we started with a capital of $20,000 when we began our option selling system in April and in just a little over five months this has ballooned to a cash position of $33,635, an increase of 68 percent! One heck of a way to make your wealth grow, don't you agree!? One could argue that it is not exactly correct to say that our trading activities returned 68% in five months when in fact we have potential liabilities with our naked positions running for another fifteen to eighteen months. But if we did nothing else in the next three months to the end of December let's see what we would have ended up with.

On December 31st QQQQ was trading at $40.33 and if we closed out all our open positions at that time, here's what it would have looked like:

Closed the three Jan 35 puts (2003) at $3.60	-$1,080
Closed the six Jan 30 puts (2003) at $2.10	- 1,260
Closed the six Jan 30 puts (2004) at $3.00	- 1,800
Cost of all closed positions	- 4,140

Taking out $4,140 from our account balance of $33,635 will leave us with a net balance of $29,495 in the account and no open positions to worry about. In real terms our initial $20,000 investment in the option selling program yielded an actual return of 47%!!

And this is not even counting the money pulled in by the other side of the option selling program; the selling of call options. Even if we were somewhat more cautious on the call side it still could have easily brought in $4,000 to $5,000. Add this to our $29,495 ending account balance and this all adds up to nearly 70% total return. All in a period of barely eight months of trading, April to December! I'm not suggesting that you should aim and expect this kind of returns all the time. The trading period covered in this exercise can be described as a very turbulent period for the stock market. Because of this high volatility option premiums were extremely high thus we achieved remarkable returns. But you can be assured you can get fantastic returns in the option selling business using my strategy of selling naked options coupled with a modified credit ratio spread and making full use of the roll out feature. In the succeeding chapter you will again see actual trading transactions of more recent dates where option premiums were not quite as high as those shown in this chapter. You will see that the returns after several months of trading are still extraordinarily good even with reduced premiums.

In closing this chapter let me hasten to say that in the option selling business you should always try and stay away from a wildly fluctuating market such as the one used in the above exercise. I only used this period to demonstrate in an exaggerated manner how you can protect yourself in this kind of market. Ideally, if you are thinking of getting into the option selling business in a safe way, and I underscore safe way, you should do so in a more stable market where price gyrations are kept to the minimum. Refrain from trading when the market starts to move swiftly in one direction, either up or down. If this happens and you are already caught in the middle of the game try and extricate yourself by making good use of the roll out process with the objective of exiting the market when possible. DON'T OPEN NEW SHORT POSITIONS. Stay on the sidelines until the market behaves more rationally and volatility is at more normal levels. High volatility can be good and bad for the option seller. Good in that it provides excellent options prices but bad in that it can cause wild price gyrations and could lead to a continuing trend in one direction which in turn could put your option positions deep ITM.

One last fatherly advice. For those getting into the option selling business for the first time, I strongly recommend doing only puts. Stay away from selling naked calls! Trading in naked calls is advised only if and when you have acquired enough experience and skill trading naked puts.

CHAPTER EIGHT

Looking over my shoulder with trading bulletins

This may be the most valuable chapter in this book. This book as it appears today is the end product of what I initially produced as a short e-book back in 2007. That e-book version was quite brief in content and was offered as some kind of a "how to" manual explaining my option selling system to visitors of my web site. Although brief it did contain all the trading illustrations shown in Chapter Five of this book. As more and more people got to read the e-book I began getting requests from readers who obviously were serious options enthusiasts asking for some kind of service where they could see and follow my actual trading activities. Moreover, many readers wanted to see how I handled trading both calls and puts using my strategy. Since the e-book touched only on trading naked puts as illustrated in Chapter Five for reasons stated in that chapter, many readers wanted to see in actual play how naked trading in calls and puts can be done simultaneously and effectively. I eventually came out with a bulletin service where for a nominal monthly subscription fee I would email my trades to subscribers immediately as and when I made my option trades. The trading bulletin service in effect offered subscribers an opportunity to look over my shoulder as I did my trades.

In order to enable subscribers to follow my trades every step of the way I created real portfolios with real funds in my options account with my broker. Listed below is one of the portfolios that were created and traded during the time that my trading bulletin was active. Every trade was accompanied with a commentary explaining the reasons why I was doing what I was doing. The trades shown here will prove to be immensely valuable to the reader since these are actual trades that were witnessed by a large following of subscribers. In your learning process I sincerely hope these trades will be as useful to you as it had been to the people that traded with me during these times.

I started the bulletin service in February of 2009 by setting aside $10,000 in my broker account to use exclusively for the trading bulletin service. This was to serve as my first Trading Bulletin Portfolio which I named Portfolio 209. All the dates mentioned are in 2009. What you see below are the exact reprints of my trading bulletins that were emailed to subscribers on the dates shown.

Feb 9 – Today I set up a new portfolio with an initial capitalization of $10,000. I placed my first trades for this portfolio as shown below using the ETF stock iShares:Russell 2000 Index (symbol IWM) when the stock was at a price of $46.40:

sold to open 18 contracts of March		
Q1 53 call @ 0.61	=	1,098.00
sold to open 18 contracts of March		
Q1 38 put @ 0.82	=	1,476.00
total cash intake	=	2,574.00
Portfolio cash position today	=	12,574.00

The margin requirement for the above trade is approximately $7,700

My choice of strike prices for the calls and puts is strictly a personal one based on my risk tolerance and desired return on my investment. You will note my chosen strike prices are quite farther out from the current underlying's price as opposed to what my book recommends. The reason for this is that the current market situation is highly volatile and there is too much uncertainty in the market. For the same reason of uncertainty in the market I chose the shorter March expirations in order not to expose myself to the greater risk of selling longer term options. I would have considered April expirations if these were available but they were not. For the more conservative options trader the March 54 or 55 calls together with the 37 or 36 puts would have still yielded decent returns at the same time providing greater protection against the volatility of the market.

I will now wait and see how the market pans out and hopefully be able to construct my modified ratio spread in the coming days. If IWM's price rises or drops by say more than 3% in the comings days I should be able to create my spread. In a downtrend I would be looking to buy 7 contracts of the March 49 or 50 calls at less than $1.00. In an uptrend I would look for the March 41 or 42 puts priced at less than $1.30 to buy 7 contracts. This is assuming there is a significant market move within the next week. My price buying objectives will be adjusted accordingly if there is no significant market action in more than a week. I will keep my subscribers posted of any changes in plans.

<u>**NOTE:**</u> In this book I suggested that one should avoid trading naked options in a volatile market. I'm here breaking this sound advice for the benefit of traders who insist on trading in any kind of market with the hope that it will show them how to handle volatile situations just like I did in Chapter Five.

<u>**Feb 10**</u> – I didn't have to wait long. Today the market took a dive with IWM dropping in price to $44.68. This opened up an opportunity to create a ratio spread on the call side. Here's the trade I did today:

Bought to open 7 contracts of March		
Q1 50 calls @ 0.99	=	693.00
Portfolio cash position today	=	11,881.00

The 18 contracts of March 53 short calls are now partially covered by the 7 long calls thereby releasing margin funds that I can use to increase my inventory of short calls. But I decided not to increase my present short positions for the time being. I will wait to see how the market behaves in the following days and make a decision then. I'm hoping the market will shortly reverse itself and rise to the same level as previously or even higher. In this event I will again sell calls and, depending on how far IWM's price rises, I may also create a spread on the put side, buying puts to partially cover the short puts.

Feb 18 – Today IWM's price deteriorated and closed at $42.29. This has caused my March Q1 38 puts to appreciate in price to a point that increases the maintenance margin requirement. I may be called to increase my margin deposit. To avoid this I will plan to roll out the March 38 puts if tomorrow IWM's price drops to less than $42. This is my plan of action tomorrow. Buy to close the 18 contracts of March 38 puts at around $1.80 and roll out by selling 14 contracts of June Q2 36 puts at around $2.50 or better. Doing this would reduce my put contracts thereby reducing the maintenance margin. With this transaction I would avoid being called for additional funds but still gain a little positive cash flow in the process. In this instance I'm rolling out not because the underlying's price has reached my strike price but I'm doing so to reduce the maintenance margin requirement. This is yet another useful feature of the roll out strategy. In retrospect I should not have sold so many put contracts when I initiated the strangle on Feb 9th. Instead of the original 18 contracts I should have only done 16 contracts or maybe 15. But I'm glad I did because this gives my readers an opportunity to learn how to cope with the potential menace of being called for additional margin. Let's see what happens tomorrow. Stay tuned.

Feb 19 – Yep, IWM dipped down to below $42! At the price of 41.93 I rolled out by buying to close the 18 contracts of March Q1 38 puts and sold to open 11 contracts of the June Q2 36 puts. Why did I sell only 11 June puts instead of the 14 that I mentioned yesterday? Following my strategy of reducing contracts at roll outs the less contracts sold the better. With the market now in a continuous downtrend it makes sense at this point to reduce the naked puts. This transaction has not only reduced my naked position on the put side, it has also reduced the margin requirement significantly as this now stands at less than $6,000. At the same time this transaction also generated a positive cash flow in the amount of $261. Here's how my cash position stands:

2/9	Beginning balance	10,000.00
2/09	sold to open 18 contracts of March Q1 53 calls @ 0.61	1,098.00
2/09	sold to open 18 contracts of March Q1 38 put @ 0.82	1,476.00
2/10	Bought to open 7 contracts of March Q1 50 calls @ 0.99	- 693.00
2/19	bought to close 18 March Q1 38 puts @ 1.34	-2,412.00
2/19	sold to open 11 June Q2 36 puts @ 2.43	2,673.00
	Cash position today	12,142.00

I now find myself in a fairly comfortable position in regards to my portfolio and, unless and until IWM's price drops by more than 10% I won't be taking any action for the next few days. I will look at the whole picture again on Monday or Tuesday. Meanwhile you may not hear from me till then.

Feb 23 – A down day in the market today with IWM closing at 39.56. In reviewing my positions I see there may be some pressure on my maintenance margin once again. Although at the current price of IWM I'm still within the margin requirements I've decided that tomorrow I will close out my calls just to be on the safe side. Anyhow, the short calls are at such a low price now that it does not make sense to keep margin money tied up to support it. I will place a buy order to close the 18 March Q1 53 calls at $0.05. Hopefully some time later in the week we shall see some kind of an uptick in the market. I should then be in a good position to sell new calls. I will hang on to the long calls since there is little sense in closing these as they would bring in very little cash. I would much rather keep them for, who knows, the market might just decide to reverse and these calls would then be worth more than what they are today. After all, they still have a whole month to go before expiration.

Feb 24 – Even with the run up in price at $41.02 I went ahead and bought to close the 18 MarchQ1 calls at $0.05. Here's my position at the end of today:

Last cash position on 2/19	=	12,142.00
Bought to close 18 MarchQ1 calls @ $0.05	=	-90.00
Cash position today	=	12,052.00

The plan tomorrow is to sell new call options. I'm looking at possibly selling 7 April 46 calls at around $0.95. I may decide to decrease my target price if the market shows weakness after today's run-up.

Feb 25 – My plan of selling 7 contracts of April 46 calls at $$0.95 was too ambitious. Instead I compromised by selling 7 April 45 calls at $.85 when IWM was at $40.45. The stock went up to as high as 41.07 before dropping and finally closing at 40.17. After today's transaction I have no action plans for the following days unless IWM makes a dramatic move upwards in which case I may sell more calls and hopefully create a ratio spread on the short puts. My cash position today:

2/9	Beginning balance	10,000.00
2/09	sold to open 18 contracts of March Q1 53 calls @ 0.61	1,098.00
2/09	sold to open 18 contracts of March Q1 38 put @ 0.82	1,476.00

2/10	Bought to open 7 contracts of March Q1 50 calls @ 0.99	- 693.00
2/19	Bought to close 18 March Q1 38 puts @ (1.34	-2,412.00
2/19	sold to open 11 June Q2 36 puts @ 2.43	2,673.00
2/24	bought to close 18 MarchQ1 53 calls @ $0.05	-90.00
2/25	sold to open 7 April 45 calls @ .85	595.00
	Cash position today	12,647.00

March 2 – A bad day in the markets today. In tandem with the downtrend IWM closed at $36.94 bringing it very close to my June Q2 puts. If tomorrow the price drops further I will proceed to roll out the June Q2 36 puts. I will wait to see if IWM continues to slide down to 36.45 or less and if it does I will buy to close the 11 contracts of June 36 Q2 puts at the ask price and roll out by selling to open 8 of the January 30/2011 puts at the bid price. Additionally, if the April 45 calls drop to a price of .20 I may either create a ratio spread or just buy back to close some of the contracts.

This crazy market has now dropped about 20% from the time I opened this portfolio. This is a very steep decline in the very short period of only three trading weeks. The present condition is wreaking havoc on values of almost all kinds of investment portfolios. It is worth mentioning that my portfolio 209 seems to be holding quite well in the face of this onslaught.

March 3 – As planned I bought to close the 11 June Q2 36 puts at $4.35 when IWM was at 36.30. I rolled out and sold 8 Jan 2011 puts with strike 30 for $6.00. Here is my position today:

2/10	Bought to open 7 contracts of March Q1 50 calls @ 0.99	- 693.00
2/19	bought to close 18 March Q1 38 puts @ (1.34	-2,412.00
2/19	sold to open 11 June Q2 36 puts @ 2.43	2,673.00

2/24	bought to close 18 MarchQ1 53 calls @ $0.05	-90.00
2/25	sold to open 7 April 45 calls @ .85	595.00
3/3	bought to close 11 June Q2 36 puts @ 4.35	4,785.00
3/3	sold to open 8 contracts Jan/2011 30 puts @ 6.00	4,800.00
	Current position	12,662.00

IWM closed at $36.24 today. At this point there are no more future puts that I can roll out to if IWM continues its downward slide. I don't see this as too big of a problem though. Assuming the price drops down to 30, the strike of my Jan 2011 puts, it would not likely be assigned since it's too far out in the future. In all probability no assignment will happen till the price goes farther down to way below 30 and it is unlikely the entire 8 contract will be assigned. More likely two or three contracts may be assigned and at $30 (the strike price at which I would be assigned) I don't mind buying the stock.

Now here's another strategy for those who want to get completely out of the risk of being assigned if the price drops to $30. Buy to close the 8 put contracts and sell to open enough options of an index with European style expiration. For those of you not familiar with European style options, these options cannot be exercised or assigned until expiration date. This means you need not worry about being assigned no matter how low the price drops for as long as the strike is far away into the future. With strike prices 18 or 24 months away, chances are that the stock market will rebound by the time the options expire. If prices don't rebound when there are only a few weeks to expiration you can again roll out the European options farther and escape assignment. With only a few weeks left in the life of the options there is very little time value left and you would be buying at a very much depreciated price and rolling out to new much higher prices or, just close them out at the reduced price. The following are European type options:

MID - S&P Midcap 400 Index
MNX - Mini-NDX Index
NDX - Nasdaq-100 Index
DJX - Dow Jones Industrial Index
RUT - Russell 2000 Index
SPX - S&P 500 Index
XEO - S&P 100 Index

March 6 – For all the doom and gloom reported in the news today the markets seem to have stood firm. Are we finally reaching bottom? If the weekend and Monday bring more bad news yet the markets do not go into another free fall it may be a good sign. I may close out the April 45 calls if I can get a price of $0.10 or less. And later in the trading session, say about 30 minutes before closing time and assuming the markets continue to hold, I will open a new short call position by selling 8 contracts of April 39 or 40 calls at a price of at least $0.85.

March 9 – Another down day for the stock market! I closed the April 45 calls at $0.08 earlier in the day when IWM was at $34.91. I put off my plan of selling new calls being fearful that with so many days of downtrend I could be facing a potential major correction in the market. I don't want to get caught with newly sold calls when/if the market suddenly reverses. I will sit a while and see what happens the rest of this week.

Due to the long and extended downward trend in the market PORTFOLIO 209 is now reaching a near stagnation point where there may be little action in the coming weeks. I'm thinking of opening a new portfolio, perhaps in the next two weeks, to give readers an opportunity to see fresh action in a newly developing portfolio.

March 10 - After yesterday's down day I thought I wouldn't be doing much action on this portfolio for a while. The market certainly did a remarkable turnaround today! I therefore proceeded with my earlier plan of selling new calls. With IWM up at 36.51 I sold 8 contracts of April 40 calls at $.82. Here is this portfolio's position as of today:

2/24	bought to close 18 MarchQ1 53 calls @ $0.05	-90.00
2/25	sold to open 7 April 45 calls @ .85	595.00
3/3	bought to close 11 June Q2 36 puts @ 4.35	-4,785.00
3/3	sold to open 8 contracts Jan/2011 30 puts @ 6.00	4,800.00
3/9	bought to close 7 April 45 calls @ .08	-56.00
3/10	sold to open 8 April 40 calls @ $.82	656.00

March 12 – The bulls seem to have awakened and are on the charge. I will wait to see what happens in the next two to three trading days before doing anything. But if tomorrow there is another run-up like today and IWM's price hits my April 40 strike I will have to roll it farther out.

March 13 – Market was up again today but not high enough for IWM to hit my April 40 strike price. After four days of gains and being the last day of the week I decided not to roll out even though IWM hovered close to 40. I will see what Monday brings. Chances are we should see a correction early next week in view of this week's gains. After all we are still in deep recession.

March 16 – I rolled out the 8 contracts April 40 calls to 5 contracts of Dec Q4 (2009) 44 calls when IWM was at a price of $40.04. Current position:

2/25	sold to open 7 April 45 calls @ .85	595.00
3/3	bought to close 11 June Q2 36 puts @ 4.35	-4,785.00
3/3	sold to open 8 contracts Jan/2011 30 puts @ 6.00	4,800.00
3/9	bought to close 7 April 45 calls @ .08	-56.00
3/10	sold to open 8 April 40 calls @ $.82	656.00
3/16	bought to close 8 April 40 calls @ 2.12	-1,696.00
3/16	sold to open 5 Dec Q4 (2009) 44 calls @ 3.65	1,825.00

My current open positions of 8 short puts and 5 short calls allow me to write new calls and puts and still be within maintenance margin requirements. I will observe how the market behaves in the next day or two before deciding to open new positions. I will also be creating a new portfolio later this week (Portfolio 309) for the benefit of new subscribers who didn't catch the beginning action of Portfolio 209

March 20 – With IWM at a price of $40.07 I sold 5 contracts May 35 puts at $1.34.

3/3	sold to open 8 contracts Jan/2011 30 puts @ 6.00	4,800.00
3/9	bought to close 7 April 45 calls @ .08	-56.00
3/10	sold to open 8 April 40 calls @ $.82	656.00
3/16	bought to close 8 April 40 calls @ 2.12	-1,696.00
3/16	sold to open 5 Dec Q4 (2009) 44 calls @ 3.65	1,825.00
3/20	sold to open 5 May 35 puts @ 1.34	670.00

As of today I have the following open positions:

7 March Q1 50 calls (now has zero value and will almost surely expire worthless)
5 Dec 44 Q4/09 calls
8 Jan 30, 2011 puts
5 May 35 puts

The maintenance margin for all the above is less than $7,000 thereby allowing me to write more puts and even more calls if I should decide to do so. I may write more puts next week depending on how the market behaves. If the market continues to drop I may be able to create a ratio spread on the Dec calls by buying 2 Dec 40 or 41 calls.

Meanwhile the creation of a new portfolio which was planned for this week has been delayed due to slight problems in setting up a new account with another broker. This will be Portfolio 309 and will be funded with $14,000 capitalization.

<u>March 23</u> – An incredible upward move in the market today! Here are my plans for tomorrow:

Roll in the 8 Jan 30/2011 puts by buying them at a price of $4.50-$4.65 and sell to open 6 Jan 40/2011 puts at $6.35-6.50. I've put this order at the close of trading today with the expectation that it would be filled at the opening bell tomorrow. My order on the buy side is at $4.50 and the sell side at $6.50.

At the same time I also put in an order to buy 2 May 39 puts at $1.45 to create the long side of a ratio spread on my short May 35 puts.

I should also do a roll out of the Dec 44 calls but the spread between the bid and ask prices are so ridiculously wide as to not permit me to do a decent roll out. I will wait and see what happens and then decide. Another alternative is to convert the calls to puts where the premiums are more reasonable. I'll wait and see what happens in following days.

<u>March 24</u> - Here are my trades today:

bought to close 8 Jan 30/11 puts @ 4.10	=	-3,280.00
sold to open 5 Jan 39/11 puts @ 7.25	=	3,625.00
bought to open 2 May 39 puts @1.69	=	-338.00

The first trade is a roll in together with the second trade. The long May 39 puts creates a ratio spread with my May 35 puts. Here's my current position:

3/16	bought to close 8 April 40 calls @ 2.12	-1,696.00
3/16	sold to open 5 Dec Q4 (2009) 44 calls @ 3.65	1,825.00
3/20	sold to open 5 May 35 puts @ 1.34	670.00
3/24	bought to close 8 Jan 30/11 puts @ 4.10	-3,280.00
3/24	sold to open 5 Jan 39/11 puts @ 7.25	3,625.00
3/24	bought to open 2 May 39 puts @1.69	-338.00

<u>March 26</u> – I have never in all my trading years seen the market rise as fast as it has done in the last two weeks. It has been said that this market behavior has not been seen in a hundred years. In the face of this market run up and to be on the side of caution I've decided to close my naked calls for the time being. Here is my trade today.

Previous cash position	=	14,068.00
bought to close 5 Dec Q4 44 calls @ 5.90	=	-2,950.00
Cash position today	=	11,118.00

In the naked selling game one has to be watchful when it comes to calls. Keep in mind that naked call selling has dangers that are not so inherent on the put side. This is the reason why most options brokers require clients to maintain very large cash accounts for naked call selling but allow minimal balances for naked puts.

If the market pulls back in the coming days, and it surely will, I will open new put positions in place of the closed calls and try to recover some of the loss sustained with the closing of the calls.

<u>April 8</u> – There seems to be an upward magnet that is pulling the market up even in the face of a series of continu-

ing bad news. Has the market hit bottom and is now trending upwards?

I decided to close my May 35 puts since they have now lost quite a bit of value. If the market again turns downward then I would open new put positions to replace the ones closed today.

Also, in response to what appears to be a strong upward pull in the market I've decided to do something unusual. I bought to open 2 long calls with the plan that if the market continues its upward tendency I would then create a ratio spread by selling calls against the long position. This is actually the reverse of my usual ratio spread strategy where I first sell options then leg in the long side when the market moves favorably in my direction. I made sure though that the longs have far away expirations with the idea that the market is now nearing bottom and will most likely start recovering, if not in the next few weeks, certainly in the coming months to the end of the year.

April 9 – As planned I sold to open 6 calls to complete the ratio spread with the longs I bought yesterday.

Previous cash position	=	11,118.00
4/8 – bought to close 5 May 35 puts @ .34	=	-170.00
4/8 – bought to open 2 Dec 45 calls @ 5.75	=	-1,150.00
4/9 – sold to open 6 May 50 calls @ 1.25	=	750.00
Cash position today	=	10,548.00

April 20 – With the market pulling back today I decided to open additional long calls to further improve the ratio spread on the May 50 short calls. Again I bought far away calls (Dec) in view that in the last six weeks the market showed a strong pull upwards. But if there is further deterioration in the next couple of days I may buy even more Dec calls and at the same time sell new short puts. Here is my current position:

3/26	bought to close 5 Dec Q4 44 calls @ 5.90	-2,950.00
4/8	bought to close 5 May 35 puts @ .34	-170.00
4/8	bought to open 2 Dec 45 calls @ 5.75	-1,150.00
4/9	sold to open 6 May 50 calls @ 1.25	750.00
4/20	bought to open 2 Dec 45 calls @ 6.6	-1,320.00
	Current cash position	9,228.00

April 29 - With IWM at 49.06 I sold 4 new Nov 54 calls at 1.15. These calls together with the May 50 calls form a ratio spread of 10 shorts against 4 longs. This is a nice ratio spread because the long Dec 45s are well in the money which gives them much higher value. The May 50 calls are getting near the money and if IWM continues its upward move and hits the 50 strike price I will roll them out into lesser contracts, say, 3 or 4. If this happens I may also roll the Dec 45 longs by closing them and rolling them into maybe 5 or 6 contracts of Dec 50 or Dec 49. I may even consider doing Nov 49 on 50 on the long side. Take note when rolling out short positions, I lessen the number of contracts. But when I roll out long positions that are well ITM I try to roll out into more contracts by using the profits to pay for the additional contracts.

3/26	bought to close 5 Dec Q4 44 calls @ 5.90	-2,950.00
4/8	bought to close 5 May 35 puts @ .34	-170.00
4/8	bought to open 2 Dec 45 calls @ 5.75	-1,150.00
4/9	sold to open 6 May 50 calls @ 1.25	750.00
4/20	bought to open 2 Dec 45 calls @ 6.6	-1,320.00
4/29	Sold to open 4 June 54 calls @ 1.15	460.00
	Current cash position	9,688.00

May 1 – Taking advantage of IWM's slight retreat near the end of a see-sawing trading day I sold to open 4 June 43 puts @ 1.22 when the stock was at 48.58. At the end of the trading session IWM recovered to close at 48.82 thereby giving the new short position a slight positive move.

4/8	bought to close 5 May 35 puts @ .34	-170.00
4/8	bought to open 2 Dec 45 calls @ 5.75	-1,150.00
4/9	sold to open 6 May 50 calls @ 1.25	750.00
4/20	bought to open 2 Dec 45 calls @ 6.6	-1,320.00
4/29	Sold to open 4 June 54 calls @ 1.15	460.00
5/1	Sold to open 4 June 43 puts @ 1.22	488.00
	Current cash position	10,176.00

May 4 - Just before the markets closed I rolled out the May 50 calls to Nov 55 calls and reduced the contracts from 6 to 4.

4/9	sold to open 6 May 50 calls @ 1.25	750.00
4/20	bought to open 2 Dec 45 calls @ 6.6	-1,320.00
4/29	Sold to open 4 June 54 calls @ 1.15	460.00
5/1	Sold to open 4 June 43 puts @ 1.22	488.00
5/4	Bought to close 6 May 50 calls @1.84	-1,104.00
5/4	Sold to open 4 Nov 55 calls @ 3.6	1,440.00
	Current cash position	10,512.00

May 7 – With today's market pullback I decided to add two long contracts on the call side. I bought to open 2 November 51 calls which also serve to form a ratio spread on the Jun 54 short calls. This portfolio is nicely positioned on the call side with 6 long calls having far expirations forming a ratio spread against 8 short calls with short expirations.

Taking advantage of the pullback I also opened a new short put position selling 6 June 44 puts. The cash generated on this transaction served to offset some of the costs of the purchased calls.

4/29	Sold to open 4 June 54 calls @ 1.15	460.00
5/1	Sold to open 4 June 43 puts @ 1.22	488.00
5/4	Bought to close 6 May 50 calls @1.84	-1,104.00
5/4	Sold to open 4 Nov 55 calls @ 3.6	1,440.00
5/7	Bought to open 2 Nov 51 calls @ 4.75	-950.00
5/7	Sold to open 6 June 44 puts @ 1.15	690.00
	Current cash position	10,252.00

May 21 - I took advantage of today's down market by closing the June 54 calls when IWM's price dropped to 47.61. It was nice to see it bounce back up to 48.30 by the end of the trading day. No immediate plans for this portfolio except to wait for further uptrend and then sell new call positions.

5/1	Sold to open 4 June 43 puts @ 1.22	488.00
5/4	Bought to close 6 May 50 calls @1.84	-1,104.00
5/4	Sold to open 4 Nov 55 calls @ 3.6	1,440.00
5/7	Bought to open 2 Nov 51 calls @ 4.75	-950.00
5/7	Sold to open 6 June 44 puts @ 1.15	690.00
5/21	Bought to close 4 June 54 calls @ .21	-84.00
	Current cash position	10,168.00

May 22 – It was not my plan to trade today as I was waiting for an upward movement in the market. But with the disturbing news of the US' possible credit rating downgrade I decided to add some short calls to my portfolio. These would help cushion a sudden slide in the market if this should happen next week. If instead, the market rebounds as I hope it does, the short calls won't be a drag as I have enough long call positions to cover the short calls.

5/4	Bought to close 6 May 50 calls @1.84	-1,104.00
5/4	Sold to open 4 IWM Nov 55 calls @ 3.6	1,440.00
5/7	Bought to open 2 IWM Nov 51 calls @ 4.75	-950.00
5/7	Sold to open 6 IWM June 44 puts @ 1.15	690.00
5/21	Bought to close 4 IWM June 54 calls @ .21	-84.00
5/22	Sold to open 6 IWM July 53 calls @ .88	528.00
	Current cash position	10,696.00

June 1 – The markets' large move up today presented several opportunities for trades in this portfolio. Firstly I decided to close out the short June puts since they have now lost significant values and if the market reverses in the coming days I can again open new puts. I opted to close the short puts instead of opening long puts for a ratio spread because there are only very few weeks left in them. At the same time I opened a new call position to complete a ratio spread with the November and December long calls. I now have six long calls to sixteen short calls. The Novembers are now ITM while the Decembers are deep ITM.

5/7	Bought to open 2 IWM Nov 51 calls @ 4.75	-950.00
5/7	Sold to open 6 IWM June 44 puts @ 1.15	690.00
5/21	Bought to close 4 IWM June 54 calls @ .21	-84.00
5/22	Sold to open 6 IWM July 53 calls @ .88	528.00
6/1	Bought to close 4 IWM June 43 puts @ 0.13	-52.00
6/1	Bought to close 6 IWM June 44 puts @ 0.17	-102.00
6/1	Sold to open 6 IWM July 57 calls @ .6	360.00
	Current cash position	10,902.00

June 3 – Today's market pullback offered an opportunity to sell puts. I sold 6 July IWM 45 puts when the underlying was at 52.03. It closed the day higher at 52.43. I wanted to sell more puts but I thought I'd stay on the side of caution limiting the contracts to only six with the plan that if IWM goes on another slide in the coming days I could sell another 6 contracts.

5/21	Bought to close 4 IWM June 54 calls @ .21	-84.00
5/22	Sold to open 6 IWM July 53 calls @ .88	528.00
6/1	Bought to close 4 IWM June 43 puts @ 0.13	-52.00
6/1	Bought to close 6 IWM June 44 puts @ 0.17	-102.00
6/1	Sold to open 6 IWM July 57 calls @ .6	360.00
6/3	Sold to open 6 IWM July 45 puts @ .71	426.00
	Current cash position	11,328.00

June 5 – With IWM now up to the level of my July 53 short calls and in line with my roll out strategy I decided to roll out the options to a farther date and reduce the number of contracts from 6 to 5.

5/22	Sold to open 6 IWM July 53 calls @ .88	528.00
6/1	Bought to close 4 IWM June 43 puts @ 0.13	-52.00
6/1	Bought to close 6 IWM June 44 puts @ 0.17	-102.00
6/1	Sold to open 6 IWM July 57 calls @ .6	360.00
6/3	Sold to open 6 IWM July 45 puts @ .71	426.00
6/5	Bought to close 6 IWM July 53 calls @ 2.51	-1,506.00
6/5	Sold to open 5 IWM November 56 calls @ 3.40	1,700.00
	Current cash position	11,522.00

June 15 – With the market dropping by more than 2% today I decided to sell some puts.

6/1	Bought to close 4 IWM June 43 puts @ 0.13	-52.00
6/1	Bought to close 6 IWM June 44 puts @ 0.17	-102.00
6/1	Sold to open 6 IWM July 57 calls @ .6	360.00
6/3	Sold to open 6 IWM July 45 puts @ .71	426.00
6/5	Bought to close 6 IWM July 53 calls @ 2.51	-1,506.00
6/5	Sold to open 5 IWM November 56 calls @ 3.40	1,700.00
6/15	Sold to open 5 IWM July 46 puts @ .75	375.00
	Current cash position	11,897.00

June 17 – Being a little fearful of the potential for a continued downfall in the markets I decided to close the deep in-the-money IWM Dec 45 long calls and replace these with at-the-money long calls. When options are too deep ITM such as those long Dec 45s they move more drastically in tandem with the market versus those that are ATM that move more slowly. The option is said to have a high delta which means that it will move up or down in greater parity with the underlying. Deep ITM calls are good when the market is in an uptrend but they also move faster downward in a declining market. By going ATM I was able to decrease the possibility of rapidly losing value (the option having a lower delta) in those calls should the market continue to drop. Plus I was also able to increase the number of contracts with the money obtained from the sale of the ITM calls. The increased quantity of long calls is a benefit in that it gives me the opportunity of selling more short call contracts when the opportunity arises.

6/3	Sold to open 6 IWM July 45 puts @ .71	426.00
6/5	Bought to close 6 IWM July 53 calls @ 2.51	-1,506.00
6/5	Sold to open 5 IWM November 56 calls @ 3.40	1,700.00
6/15	Sold to open 5 IWM July 46 puts @ .75	375.00
6/17	Sold to close 4 IWM Dec 45 calls @ 8.40	3,360.00
6/17	Bought to open 6 IWM Dec 51 calls @ 5.00	-3,000.00
	Current cash position	12,257.00

<u>June 21</u> – Big drop in the markets today. With the price of the July 57 calls down to a low of $0.06 I decided to buy and close them out. I will wait for a rebound and sell new short calls.

6/3	Sold to open 6 IWM July 45 puts @ .71	426.00
6/5	Bought to close 6 IWM July 53 calls @ 2.51	-1,506.00
6/5	Sold to open 5 IWM November 56 calls @ 3.40	1,700.00
6/15	Sold to open 5 IWM July 46 puts @ .75	375.00
6/17	Sold to close 4 IWM Dec 45 calls @ 8.40	3,360.00
6/17	Bought to open 6 IWM Dec 51 calls @ 5.00	-3,000.00
6/21	Bought to close 6 Jul 57 calls @ .06	-36.00
	Current cash position	12,221.00

<u>July 7</u> – For the second day today the markets have been extremely weak. I closed the Nov 55 and Nov 56 calls and hope to replace these with new September or November calls if/when the market rebounds. If IWM continues to drop I plan to close the July 45 and 46 puts and replace these with August or September puts. Having now run this portfolio for five months I'm planning to close it and perhaps start a fresh one when the opportunity arises.

6/17	Sold to close 4 IWM Dec 45 calls @ 8.40	3,360.00
6/17	Bought to open 6 IWM Dec 51 calls @ 5.00	-3,000.00
6/21	Bought to close 6 Jul 57 calls @ .06	-36.00
7/7	Bought to close 4 IWM Nov 55 calls @ 1.39	-556.00
7/7	Bought to close 5 IWM Nov 56 calls @ 1.14	-570.00
	Current cash position	11,095.00

July 8 – As I mentioned yesterday I closed the July 45 and 46 puts with the market's continued drop today. I had to close these two positions because my option buying power (which is what I use to monitor my margin requirement balance) went negative. If I did not close the positions I could have gotten a margin call by the end of the trading day or tomorrow morning. With the closure of the puts my option buying power went into positive territory. I can now sell to open 8 or more August puts and my option buying power would still be positive.

6/17	Sold to close 4 IWM Dec 45 calls @ 8.40	3,360.00
6/17	Bought to open 6 IWM Dec 51 calls @ 5.00	-3,000.00
6/21	Bought to close 6 Jul 57 calls @ .06	-36.00
7/7	Bought to close 4 IWM Nov 55 calls @ 1.39	-556.00
7/7	Bought to close 5 IWM Nov 56 calls @ 1.14	-570.00
7/8	Bought to close 6 IWM July 45 puts @ .35	-210.00
7/8	Bought to close 5 IWM July 46 puts @ .56	-280.00
	Current cash position	10,605.00

July 13 - Sold to open 5 Sept 54 calls @ .89 when IWM was @ 49.29

7/7	Bought to close 4 IWM Nov 55 calls @ 1.39	-556.00
7/7	Bought to close 5 IWM Nov 56 calls @ 1.14	-570.00

7/8	Bought to close 6 IWM July 45 puts @ .35	-210.00
7/8	Bought to close 5 IWM July 46 puts @ .56	-280.00
7/13	Sold to open 5 IWM Sept 54 calls @ .89	445.00
	Current cash position	11,050.00

<u>July 16</u> – Today I decided to close the January 39, 2011 puts as they are now too far away from the money with IWM at 52.00. I bought the 5 shorts and replaced them by selling to open 3 Jan 46, 2011 puts. My purpose here is to bring the puts closer to the current price of IWM in order to hasten the decay factor. Strikes that are too far away from the current underlying price decay more slowly than those closer to the current price. Since my trading system centers on the decaying characteristics of options it makes sense to bring strike prices closer to the underlying price, but not too close as to pose a risk of getting quickly ITM. I decreased the quantity in order not to have to put up too much margin money since the options are closer to the money. At the same time I sold some new calls to increase my short call positions against my long calls in a ratio spread formation.

7/8	Bought to close 6 IWM July 45 puts @ .35	-210.00
7/8	Bought to close 5 IWM July 46 puts @ .56	-280.00
7/13	Sold to open 5 IWM Sept 54 calls @ .89	445.00
7/16	Bought to close 5 Jan 39/2011 IWM puts @ 3.85	-1,925.00
7/16	Sold to open 3 Jan 46/2011 IWM puts @ 6.00	1,800.00
7/16	Sold to open 6 Sept (q3) 57 calls @ 0.81	486.00
	Current cash position	11,411.00

<u>July 23</u> – With IWM up past 54 today I rolled out my Sep 54 short calls to MarchQ3/2010 57 calls reducing the contracts by 1. At the same time my long calls being now ITM gained much value so I also decided to roll these out to 11

DecQ4 55 calls @4.55 and increasing the contracts by 3. The very small negative cash flow resulting from the roll out of the Sep 54-Mar 57 calls were more than offset by the positive inflow brought in by the long call roll outs by some $380. These transactions decreased my shorts by 1 (reducing my exposure) while it increased my longs by 3 (increasing my protection). As mentioned in previous updates I try to reduce my shorts when rolling out and increase my longs.

With a healthier portfolio value over-all, I decided to open new short calls and short puts as well.

7/16	Bought to close 5 Jan 39/2011 IWM puts @ 3.85	-1,925.00
7/16	Sold to open 3 Jan 46/2011 IWM puts @ 6.00	1,800.00
7/16	Sold to open 6 Sept (q3) 57 calls @ 0.81	486.00
7/23	Sold to close 2 Nov IWM 51 calls @ 5.55	1,110.00
7/23	Sold to close 6 DecQ4 IWM 51 calls @ 6.05	3,630.00
7/23	Bought to open 11 DecQ4 IWM 55 calls @ 3.95	-4,345.00
7/23	Sold to open 6 SepQ3 IWM 59 calls @ .82	492.00
7/23	Sold to open 8 SepQ3 IWM 48 puts @ .92	736.00
7/23	Bought to close 5 SepQ3 IWM 54 calls @ 3.10	-1,550.00
7/23	Sold to open 4 MarQ1/2010 IWM 57 calls @ 3.85	1,540.00
	Current cash position	13,024.00

<u>Aug 4</u> – Several trades on this portfolio today. The far away Jan 46/2011 puts have now lost much value. The strike being quite out from the current underlying's price of 56.90, the decay factor is now very slow so that it makes sense to just close it and replace the position with newer, closer strike. I also bought to open some long puts to ratio the shorts in my inventory. Here are the trades:

7/23	Sold to close 2 Nov IWM 51 calls @ 5.55	1,110.00
7/23	Sold to close 6 DecQ4 IWM 51 calls @ 6.05	3,630.00
7/23	Bought to open 11 DecQ4 IWM 55 calls @ 3.95	-4,345.00
7/23	Sold to open 6 SepQ3 IWM 59 calls @ .82	492.00
7/23	Sold to open 8 SepQ3 IWM 48 puts @ .92	736.00
7/23	Bought to close 5 SepQ3 IWM 54 calls @ 3.10	-1,550.00
7/23	Sold to open 4 MarQ1/2010 IWM 57 calls @ 3.85	1,540.00
8/4	Bought to close 3 IWM Jan 46/2011 puts @ 1.46	-438.00
8/4	Sold to open 6 IWM SepQ3 51 puts @ .83	498.00
8/4	Bought to open 3 IWM Sep@3 puts @1.61	-483.00
	Current cash position	12,601.00

Aug 7 – This portfolio has now had a long run so today I decided the time has come to close it and prepare to open a new one for the benefit of new subscribers who joined late and did not get to see the early trading action on this Portfolio. Portfolio 209 was opened on Feb 9, 2009 capitalized at $10,000. With today's closure it has ran 26 weeks, or just about 6 months. At its liquidated value of $13,428 it has achieved a nice return of 34.3%.

Here are the closing trades:

8/7	Bought to close 6 IWM SepQ3 57 calls @ 2.69	-1614.00
8/7	Bought to close 6 IWM SepQ3 59 calls @ 1.70	-1020.00
8/7	Bought to close 8 IWM SepQ3 48 puts @ .39	-312.00
8/7	Bought to close 4 IWM MarQ1 57 calls @ 5.50	-2200.00
8/7	Sold to close 11 IWM DecQ4 55 calls @ 5.4	5940.00
8/7	Sold to close 3 IWM SepQ3 54 puts @ 1.53	459.00
8/7	Bought to close 6 IWM SepQ3 51 puts @ .71	-426.00
	Current cash position	13,428

----------------- End of bulletins ------------------

After Portfolio 209 was closed I proceeded to open a new Portfolio named 209B. This Portfolio was capitalized at $13,428 which were the funds coming out of the just closed Portfolio 209. On this one I used the ETF Pro Shares Ultra QQQ which carries the trading symbol QLD. Trading began on August 10, 2009 and like Portfolio 209 I went on trading naked calls and puts, long calls and long puts as well as ratio spreads for the next 5 months. As with the previous portfolio I continued sending out my trading bulletins to subscribers detailing all my trades as they happened. This second Portfolio was eventually closed on January 8, 2010. The liquidation value, net of broker's commissions and other fees, amounted to $21,346 for a total return of 58.9%.

I continued my trading bulletin service by opening Portfolio 309 on March 6, 2010 and this time the trades consisted of two ETFs, the iShares Russell 2000 and Financial Select Sector SPDR Fund, with trading symbols IWM and XLF. Starting capital was $14,000. This portfolio ran for five and half months and was closed on August 25, 2010. The end liquidation value was $22,524 giving a yield of 60.8%.

While Portfolios 209, 209B and 309 achieved fabulous returns, don't expect that your trading results will always be like these. Two other Portfolios in my trading bulletins didn't perform as well. Portfolio 309B which was the successor to 309 ran for seven months from August 2009 to March 2010 and produced a yield of only 10.6%. Portfolio 709 that was traded almost at the same time as 309B ran from July 2009 to February 2010 and ended with a negative yield of -2.8%. One thing you must always keep in mind is that not all trades will return fantastic profits and some will even result in losses as demonstrated by the various Portfolios above. But over- all, in the naked option trading business you can be sure you will have more winning runs that losses and in the long run you will always come out ahead of the game. Under normal market conditions when volatility is at normal levels one can safely achieve annual consistent returns in excess of 30 percent.

Listed below is a table showing the portfolios that were tracked by my bulletin service and the returns that were achieved by each.

PORTFOLIO NAME	MONTH INITIATED	DURATION	STATUS	PERCENT TOTAL RETURN
Portfolio 209	Feb-09	5.9 months	Closed in August	34.30%
Portfolio 309	Mar-09	4.9 months	Closed in August	60.90%
Portfolio 709	Jul-09	7.1 months	Closed in February 2010	-2.80%
Portfolio 209B	Aug-09	5.0 months	Closed in January 2010	64.20%
Portfolio 309B	Aug-09	7.1 months	Closed in March, 2010	10.60%

I hope this book has served its purpose in educating you in the amazingly profitable world of selling stock options as an investment.

CHAPTER NINE

FREQUENTLY ASKED QUESTIONS

In the years that my original short e-book has been online I've received numerous questions concerning my trading system and the trading bulletin service of 2009-2010. I thought it would be interesting for the reader to see the kind of questions I've received in all this time.

1. **When initiating the system for the first time should I immediately do a strangle, selling puts and calls simultaneously, or should I leg in as the market moves? Is there an ideal market situation where I should do the strangle?** The ideal market situation for an initial simultaneous strangle is when the market is not showing any tendencies of either moving up or down. In other words it's in a sideways movement. Review the last twenty to thirty market trading days and make your determination based on that. If you observe the market to be trending, then it's better to leg in your first short position. When the market reverses (and it will surely reverse at some point) you can then initiate the buy side or long position to create your ratio spread as described in this book. At the same time you can also leg in the second part of your strangle by initiating an option sale or short position on the opposite side of your first short position.

EXAMPLE: If you are looking at starting my system with an ETF, say IWM (that mimic's the Russell 2000 index) you should monitor the NASDAQ and the S&P 500 and see how they have been moving in the past three to five weeks. Look at their charts for the past three to five weeks. Assuming the market has moved upward in this period of time then I would sell calls at this point. When the market reverses, then I would buy calls to serve as partial protective cover to the options I sold. At the same time I would sell puts to complete the strangle. If you chose the DIA or the index DJX, you would be following the Dow Jones market behavior. QQQQ would be following the Nasdaq market and SPY would follow the S&P 500.

But as I've cautioned in many parts of this book, I would refrain from doing naked option trades when the market is moving continuously in one direction, whether up or down. Although the trading illustrations I've presented in this book were done during severe market gyrations these are actually not ideal conditions for my trading system as the risks could be magnified.

2. **How much movement in the market should I wait for before making a trade?** Market conditions may give you some indication of when to initiate a trade based on the market's activity. I personally wait for a move of about 1.5% before I do a trade. But in an active market, I may wait for a movement of as much as 3% to 5% before making a trade.

3. **How many contracts should I do per short position?** This is a very important question. The simple answer is: do as many as you can of one issue without taxing your capital too much. As a minimum, I would recommend six contracts. The more, the better. The reason for the greater number of contracts is so that you have room to reduce the number of contracts when you do roll outs. From six contracts you could roll out and reduce to maybe five or four, and if you need to roll out again, you can reduce to say, three contracts. If you start off with only two or three contracts it would be nearly impossible to reduce the number in case of roll outs. Keep in mind that roll outs occur very frequently and this is something you need to prepare for all the time. If your operating capital is not too large you may want to limit your choices to the less expensive stock, ETF or index issues in order to permit you to write at least six contracts. In this situation avoid the high priced issues like the index SPX if

you can't do at least six contracts. The more contracts you write the easier it is to roll out to reduced quantities.

4. **In the selling process how far out-of-the-money should I go and how far away from expiration?** Review the illustrations in the book and it should give you some idea. It's really difficult to be specific on this issue as different traders will have different risk-reward tolerances. In my case, and this is purely my own choice, I look at selling options at strike prices that are six to seven percent away from the current underlying price in a market that is not so volatile. But in an active market where stock prices are fluctuating fairway frequently, I would sell options at strike prices as far as 12 to 18 percent away from the current underlying stock price. With respect to expiration dates, keep in mind the longer the expiration date the wider should be the gap between your strike price and the current underlying price.

5. **When initiating the long side to create my spread position how many contracts should I buy?** Here again, it's entirely up to you as to how much protection you wish to give your short position. I normally buy about half the number of contracts that I sold (two to one ratio) although occasionally I may do a three to one ratio. When the market has been in a trading pattern for some time, option premiums may not be too attractive and in these situations even a four to one ratio is doable.

6. **What do you do if the underlying goes against your short position before you can leg in with the long position?** Unless your position is at risk of going ITM you should do nothing. Use the roll out feature if you need to. Please review that part of the book where it describes the roll-out procedure and look at the various illustrations. If the underlying's price eventually retreats after you did the roll out, then you may consider taking a long position to protect the new short position.

7. **At what point in the process should I decide to do a roll out?** This is described in the book but here is the short answer. Generally speaking a roll-out should be done when the underlying price starts getting close to the strike price of your short position or when it hits your short strike price. I say generally speaking, because there may be situations where you may not want to do this and wait a little longer even after your short position has gone in-the-money. As you gain trading experience you will understand this, but meanwhile you may just want to follow the general rule.

8. **It seems that "rolling out the option" is simply getting into a new position to, in a sense, fill the hole of a loss. Why wouldn't one just continue with the technique of looking for shorting opportunities in more near expiration months?** Yes, rolling out in essence prevents taking a loss at that point in time and moving the risk forward to a future date. Not only is risk moved forward but it's reduced as well since we are rolling out into lesser contracts. And every time the same option is rolled out we take on lesser contracts so that eventually the risk is reduced to bare minimum or eliminated. In the meantime, if there were long options that were initiated to cover the shorts, these are gaining value as you continue the rolling process. There will eventually come a time where the long positions would have enough value to cover the losing shorts and they could all be closed with a very good possibility of ending with a profit. At worse it would result in a small manageable loss. If you don't close and roll out the option that has gone in-the-money, your losses will continue mounting as the underlying gets farther into the money. And if it goes deep enough in-the-money it would eventually be difficult to extricate yourself from the situation of having to take a big heavy loss. New short positions will not be able to generate enough premiums to cover the fast adding losses on the option that is going deep in the money. One last reason for not wanting to open new positions without closing old ones is that you may

not have enough margin power in your broker account to allow you to open new positions. Closing out old positions and reducing the number of contracts in the roll out process enables you to increase your option margin account.

9. **Do you ever get out of a losing short position?** Occasionally. Short positions that get in-the-money are always rolled out and may eventually end up being profitable if the covering long positions have gained enough value to close out both.

10. **Do you get out of winning short positions? When?** Yes and no. I always try to carry the shorts to expiration (assuming they are not in-the-money) and then close out the longs at that time if they are in-the-money. I also close winning short positions when they have lost more than 80% of their value and there is still a few weeks remaining prior to expiration. Moreover, when the long side covering a short position is deep in the money and nearing expiration, and the short side has reached the maximum limit of roll-outs (there are no more future dates to go out to) then I would close out everything in the spread when the longs are a day or two prior to expiration.

11. **ETFs are stated as a good underlying because of their relative stability, but I have seen some very volatile ETFs. Are the ETFs you mentioned more stable than most?** Since all the ETFs that are listed in the book are all index based, yes, they are quite stable and also very liquid. You want much liquidity in this system. You may also want to look at the index options which are also quite stable and have much liquidity.

12. **Do you ever have problems getting orders filled?** Never, because I limit my choices to strictly ETFs and Indexes which are extremely liquid and heavily traded.

13. **I'm a very nervous trader and have difficulty pushing myself to open a naked position. How about if I use credit**

ratio spreads at the onset instead of being purely naked? Yes, absolutely. I myself occasionally do ratio credit spreads at the onset instead of going purely naked. I do so when there is much volatility in the market and prices are moving up and down significantly. I also do ratio credit spreads when I already have enough naked positions say, in the call side, and there is yet another opportunity to open a new call position. In order not to expose myself to too many naked calls I would then create a ratio credit spread in this instance so I'm partially protected. Be sure though that you are creating a ratio credit spread where you buy a certain number of long options at a strike near the money and sell a larger number of short options at a strike farther away from the long options you just bought. The number of longs and shorts should be such that you end up with a positive credit in your account. As to how much credit you want depends on how much safety cover you want your longs to protect your shorts. Doing ratio credit spreads at the onset of your strangle is certainly a good conservative approach. The only negative to this strategy is that in a sideways market where there is not much movement in stock prices and volatility is low with corresponding low option premiums credit ratio spreads may significantly reduce your ROIs over the long term. If you feel comfortable with potentially reducing your returns from this strategy then go for it. It will still be a far better investment trading system than many other option trading strategies.

14. **How would your method fare in an absurdly gyrating market such as that of September, October 2008?** That was an educational experience for me and it gave me a good opportunity to test my trading system in that kind of environment. Truthfully, in such a chaotic market there probably isn't one trading system that could be counted on to do a positive consistent performance. If you were caught with naked open positions when the market took those mind-boggling dives there was not much you could do but make the most of the roll

out strategy. In the roll out process try and reduce your open positions even if you must take some losing trades. In those times of high volatility where options are commanding high premiums, doing credit ratio spreads is a very good strategy. Additionally, with high option premiums it affords you the opportunity of selling far out of the money options as a safeguard against rapid and deep surges in the market.

15. **In the once-in-a-hundred-year market downturn of September-November 2008, what do you do when you have rolled out and there are no more leaps available to roll out to?** This is perhaps the one rare occasion in my trading system when you don't have much choice but to bite the bullet and take your losses as early in the game as possible. In the kind of market that drops so swiftly and deeply as has not been seen in a hundred years such as that of September to November 2008, there are no winners. It becomes a game of who loses the least and I'm confident that those using my system would stand to lose much less than other stock and option trading systems.

16. **I just purchased your ebook yesterday (May 25, 2009) and I was surprised and disappointed to see that QQQQ,s premiums today (puts & calls) are much below your examples. While I understand your stats are 8 years old how do you explain these huge differences in premiums?** The option tables pictured in my ebook are actual tables of option chain prices for QQQQ for that period. Yes, QQQQ option prices today are nowhere near those prevailing then. There are dozens of ETF stocks out there with good premiums and you should not confine yourself to just looking at QQQQ just because it was used in the book's illustrations. When I wrote my first ebook back then QQQQ was a great choice and one that I was very much involved with. But the situation is far different today and you should search for stock issues that meet your investment goals in today's global investment environment.

The questions and answers below were from subscribers to my trading bulletin service who "looked over my shoulder" as they followed my trading activity:

Q – With the market dropping so incredibly fast recently (February 9 – March 9, 2009), how will you deal with the Jan/2011 puts in your Portfolio 209? Are you going to be locked in and hope for a very modest return between now and Jan/2011? The market will sooner or later reach a bottom and go on a horizontal trend for a good many weeks if not months in tandem with the global recession. During this period we can go on to sell new call positions and this will continue to generate revenues for the portfolio. At the same time the value of the puts will erode, eventually allowing us to sell new puts. Additionally, if the market starts rebounding significantly we can then pull back our Jan 2011 put options by rolling them in which is the reverse of the roll-out process. As the price of IWM rises (and our puts go farther away from the money) we can buy back the Jan 2011 puts at a lower price and roll these to a nearer date and nearer the money position, say Jan 2010 or thereabouts. As the market continues to improve we can keep on rolling-in. At the absolutely very worst scenario where the market stays flat for the next two years, and we do the idiotic thing of doing nothing (not sell any calls and puts even though the market is flat), the Jan 2011 puts would eventually lose all its value. We would then end up with $12,662 in cash in our broker account (see latest cash position on the March 3 update). This is a return of 26.6% on our original $10,000 investment. Is this a bad return over two years when everybody has lost tremendous amounts of money? Think of the buy-and-hold investor who thought that IWM at $46.40 (price when we started Portfolio 209) was a steal when he entered the market. Let's fast forward to two years and assume IWM is still at around $33, he's lost nearly 30% of the value of his original investment versus our gain of 26.6%! And this is the absolute worst scenario for us!! Investors in equity mutual funds and most all 401K investors would be in the same situation. The covered call player, despite all the hype about this trading strategy, would be in similar situation. Perhaps not as bad, but nowhere near as good as the performance of Portfolio 209.

Q - Would you estimate that 90% of the time you have the opportunity to place both the long calls and long puts before you have to rollout one of your short positions due to the price of the underlying hitting one of your strike prices? Or would it 75% or 50%? What would you estimate? It's very difficult to quantify my answer in percentage terms. This is entirely dependent on market movement after the strangle is initiated. In my Portfolio 209 the market took a relentless downward trend very shortly after initiating the trade, consequently I did not get the chance to create a ratio credit spread.

Q - I assume you are saying that most of the time, i.e. well more than 1/2 the time, you can place both longs on for 2 credit spreads before you have to rollout of a bad position, correct? Yes, I guess you could say that in a horizontal moving market.

Q - If the underlying ETF is in a trend, instead of horizontal, is it worth trying to put a ratio credit spread on at all? You probably will only get one long option trade put on (that is, 1 credit spread). Also, if you get stopped out and then roll out then the long position you had put on is probably going to wind up worthless cause the ETF move was in 1 direction only. I'm a firm believer of the saying: "the stock market is a random walk down Wall Street". It has a mind of its own and despite all the efforts of all the geniuses in the world no one can foretell with much accuracy how the market will behave. With this in mind I always create a ratio spread whenever the opportunity arises as a form of insurance measure against the whimsical behavior of the market. Many times the long side of the ratio spread has ended with a profit thereby contributing to the over-all performance of the trade.

Q - You wrote a "horizontal market", did you mean the underlying stock? Or do you consider a trending stock in the same direction as the trending market the only way to trade a trend. I'm probably not explaining myself well. I used to only trade stocks trending in the same direction as the market BUT with ETF's I didn't think that should be a consideration, what do you think? By horizontal market I meant the movement of the underlying in particular. But since I trade mostly ETFs I may as well say the horizontal behavior of the sector represented by the ETF.

Q - I understand that creating a credit spread can be an insurance policy against a big gap move. Of course ETF's should be a lot safer than an individual stock from having a bad gap but of course, still it can happen. I wonder, have you ever run numbers on your trades to see if you've made money over time by buying the long options for credit trades as opposed to just selling puts and calls and no long positions? Or do you think the insurance has been a break even over the years? I don't really have numbers that could serve as statistical data. The ratio spread approach is just one more safety feature in my trading system that I have found to be quite effective in my years selling options. Of course, not covering your shorts with ratio longs will provide better returns on your trades, but here again is where you are facing the old adage "the greater the return, the greater the risk". Over all, this strategy has been good to me. There have also been several instances where on expiration day the underlying's price ended up being between my shorts and longs. The shorts expired worthless while the longs were closed for some value as they were then ITM. Whenever I create a ratio spread I always look at the long side as insurance cost, not expecting it to be recovered. So when the underlying ends up being mid way between my shorts and longs at expiration, then the long side comes back as recovered cost or extra revenue. The other consideration is that by opening a long position against your short position, even though with lesser contracts, you are reducing your maintenance requirement on the short side thus enabling you to open new short positions, adding diversification to your over-all portfolio.

Q - My SPY put (which I have 5 contracts of March 81 @7.71 is in the money , (SPY is at around 75). Is it not better to wait and let time value decay lower the price of the SPY before I roll to April or May or June? I would run the chance of being exercised but doesn't that happen in the last week of expiration month? And I would roll down and out the week before that. If it's an American type option exercise can happen at any time that an option gets in the money. European type options can't get exercised until expiration date. Your March 81 contract is deep enough in the money that it could be assigned long before expiration if the holder chose to do so. It is not correct to assume that options are exercised only in the last week prior to expiration. Exercise may happen at any time that an option gets in the money. If you wait for decay to diminish the cost of the option, the market may just continue to decline in which case the option price or premium will just keep going up eventually making it difficult to be rolled out without losing much.

Q - Do you have a formula you use to determine a strike price and what price you're willing to pay to buy the long side of your spread? Or do you base it on the net credit amount you want? Just wondered if you have any other guidelines that I should consider when establishing the spread. No, I don't have a formula but I would normally buy two to four strike prices away (or even more if possible) from my short position. The wider the gap the more protection you get. You are correct in saying that it is based on your goal of how much credit you wish to end up with in the event that both the short and long positions expire worthless.

Q - In your system, you roll out with less contracts and a credit, this requires you to roll out to much further months. Have you considered rolling with same number of contracts so that we do not need to roll so far out (i.e. is rolling out with less contracts critical?) My trading system works best with option durations of four weeks up to twelve weeks. This is the time span when erosion of option values gains momentum. Since time decay is our ally we would like to keep our contracts within this period as much as possible. Rolling out past the twelve week expiration would result in the options decaying more slowly than the shorter ones. If I had to roll out from say, 12 original contracts down to 8 contracts and then again from 8 contracts down to 5 then this would give me the opportunity of selling 6 or 7 new contracts with expirations of four to twelve weeks thereby giving me the opportunity of keeping some contracts within the ideal time period.

Q - While the cash position is positive, am I correct that the net liquidating value currently is a loss after taking into account the value of the open positions? Yes, that is correct. In the option selling business you won't see a positive net worth shortly after opening new positions. Under normal market conditions option selling is a strategy where time is our ally and the older the portfolio gets the better its market value. Unfortunately under the current wildly fluctuating market where we are seeing swings of as much as 10% up or down within a matter of days instead of weeks or months we are having to roll out options before they have had much time to lose value. While Portfolio 209 presently has a negative net worth, in much the same way as the entire market, it is slowly gaining value and in time will show a positive net worth. Keep in mind my option selling system does not deliver quick rewards in a short period of time but is a long term investment plan that brings positive results over a longer time span.

LIST OF OPTIONABLE STOCKS, ETFs & INDEXES

STOCKS

COMPANY NAME	SYMBOL
A. Schulman Inc.	SHLM
A123 Systems Inc.	AONE
AAR Corp.	AIR
Aarons Inc.	AAN
Abaxis Inc.	ABAX
ABB Ltd.	ABB
Abbott Labs	ABT
Abercrombie & Fitch Co.	ANF
ABIOMED Inc.	ABMD
AbitibiBowater Inc.	ABH
ABM Industries Inc	ABM
Abovenet Inc.	ABVT
Acacia Research Corp. - Acacia Techs.	ACTG
Acadia Realty Trust REIT	AKR
Accenture Ltd. Class A	ACN
ACCO Brands Corp.	ABD
Accretive Health Inc.	AH
Accuray Inc.	ARAY
Accuride Corp.	ACW
ACE Ltd.	ACE
Aceto Corp.	ACET
ACI Worldwide Inc.	ACIW
Acme Packet Inc.	APKT
Acorda Therapeutics Inc.	ACOR

Activision Blizzard Inc.	ATVI
Actuant Corp.	ATU
Actuate Corp.	BIRT
Acuity Brands Inc.	AYI
Acxiom Corp.	ACXM
Adecoagro SA	AGRO
Adobe Systems Inc.	ADBE
ADTRAN Inc.	ADTN
Advance America Cash Advance Centers Inc.	AEA
Advance Auto Parts Inc.	AAP
Advanced Energy Industries	AEIS
Advanced Magnetics Inc.	AMAG
Advanced Micro Devices Inc.	AMD
Advanced Semiconductor Engineering Inc.	ASX
Advantage Energy Income Fund	AAV
Advent Software	ADVS
AECOM Technology Corp.	ACM
Aegean Marine Petroleum Network Inc.	ANW
Aegon NV ADR	AEG
AerCap Holdings NV	AER
Aeroflex Holding Corp.	ARX
Aeropostale Inc.	ARO
AeroVironment Inc.	AVAV
AES Corp.	AES
Aetna Inc.	AET
Affiliated Mgrs. Gp.	AMG
Affymax Inc.	AFFY
Affymetrix Inc.	AFFX
AFLAC Inc.	AFL
AGCO Corp.	AGCO

Agilent Tech. Corp.	A
AGL Resources Inc.	AGL
Agnico-Eagle Mines Ltd.	AEM
Agree Realty Corp.	ADC
Agrium Inc.	AGU
Air Lease Corp.	AL
Air Methods Corp.	AIRM
Air Products & Chemicals Inc.	APD
Air Transport Services Group Inc.	ATSG
Aircastle Ltd.	AYR
Airgas Inc.	ARG
Aixtron AG	AIXG
AK Steel Hldg. Corp.	AKS
Akamai Tech. Inc.	AKAM
Akorn Inc.	AKRX
Alaska Air Group Inc.	ALK
Alaska Comms. Sys. Grp. Inc.	ALSK
Albany International Corp.	AIN
Albany Molecular Research Inc.	AMRI
Albemarle Corp.	ALB
Alberto-Culver Co. Inc.	ACV
Alcatel-Lucent	ALU
ALCOA Inc.	AA
Alere Inc.	ALR
Alerian MLP	AMLP
Alexander & Baldwin	ALEX
Alexandria Real Estate Equities Inc.	ARE
Alexco Resource Corp.	AXU
Alexion Pharma. Inc.	ALXN
Align Tech. Inc.	ALGN

Alkermes Inc.	ALKS
Allegheny Techs. Inc.	ATI
Allegiant Travel Company	ALGT
Allergan Inc.	AGN
ALLETE Inc.	ALE
Alliance Data Systems Corp.	ADS
Alliance Holdings GP L.P.	AHGP
Alliance Resource Partners LP	ARLP
AllianceBernstein Holding LP	AB
Alliant Energy Corp.	LNT
Alliant Techsystems Inc.	ATK
Allianz SE	AZSEY
Allied Nevada Gold Corp.	ANV
Allied World Assurance Company Holdings Ltd.	AWH
Allot Communications Ltd.	ALLT
Allscripts Healthcare Solutions Inc.	MDRX
Allstate Corp.	ALL
Almost Family Inc.	AFAM
Alnylam Pharma. Inc.	ALNY
Alon USA Energy Inc.	ALJ
Alpha Natural Resources Inc.	ANR
Altera Corp.	ALTR
Alterra Capital Holdings Ltd.	ALTE
Altisource Portfolio Solutions SA	ASPS
Altra Holdings Inc.	AIMC
Altria Group Inc.	MO
Alumina Ltd.	AWC
Aluminum Corp. of China Ltd.	ACH
AM Castle & Co.	CAS
Amarin Corp. plc	AMRN

Amazon.com Inc.	AMZN
AMB Property Corp.	AMB
AMCOL International Corp.	ACO
Amdocs Ltd.	DOX
Amedisys Inc.	AMED
AMERCO	UHAL
Ameren Corp.	AEE
Ameresco Inc.	AMRC
America Movil S.A. de C.V.	AMX
American Assets Trust Inc.	AAT
American Axle & Manuf. Hldgs. Inc.	AXL
American Campus Comms. Inc.	ACC
American Capital Agency Corp.	AGNC
American Capital Strategies Ltd.	ACAS
American Dairy Inc.	ADY
American Eagle Outfitters Inc.	AEO
American Ecology Corp.	ECOL
American Electric Power Co. Inc.	AEP
American Equity Inv. Life Hldg. Co.	AEL
American Express Co.	AXP
American Financial Group Inc.	AFG
American Greetings Corp. Class A	AM
American Intl. Group Inc.	AIG
American Med. Sys. Hlds. Inc.	AMMD
American Public Education Inc.	APEI
American Railcar Indus. Inc.	ARII
American Reprographics Co.	ARC
American Science & Engineering Inc.	ASEI
American Superconductor Corp.	AMSC
American Tower Corp.	AMT

American Vanguard Corp.	AVD
American Water Works Co. Inc.	AWK
Americas Car-Mart Inc.	CRMT
AmeriGas Partners LP	APU
Amerigon Inc.	ARGN
Amerigroup Corp.	AGP
Ameriprise Financial Inc.	AMP
Amerisafe Inc.	AMSF
AmerisourceBergen Corp.	ABC
Ameristar Casinos Inc.	ASCA
Ameritrade Hldg. Corp. Class A	AMTD
Ameron Intl. Corp.	AMN
Ametek Inc.	AME
Amgen Inc.	AMGN
Amkor Tech. Inc.	AMKR
AMN Healthcare Services Inc.	AHS
Amphenol Corp.	APH
AMR Corp.	AMR
Amsurg Corp.	AMSG
Amtech Systems Inc.	ASYS
Amtrust Financial Services Inc.	AFSI
Amylin Pharma. Inc.	AMLN
Amyris Inc.	AMRS
Anadarko Petroleum Corp.	APC
Analog Devices Inc.	ADI
Analogic Corp.	ALOG
Ancestry.com Inc.	ACOM
Andersons Inc.	ANDE
AngioDynamics Inc.	ANGO
Anglo American PLD ADR	AAUKY

Anglogold Ashanti Ltd.	AU
Anheuser-Busch InBev ADR	BUD
Anixter Intl. Inc.	AXE
Ann Taylor Stores Inc.	ANN
Annaly Mortgage Mgmt. Inc.	NLY
ANSYS Inc.	ANSS
Anworth Mortgage Asset Corp.	ANH
AO Smith Corp.	AOS
AOL Inc.	AOL
AON Corp.	AON
APAC Customer Services Inc.	APAC
Apache Corp.	APA
Apartment Inv.& Mang. Class A	AIV
Apogee Enterprises Inc.	APOG
Apollo Commercial Real Estate Finance Inc.	ARI
Apollo Global Management LLC	APO
Apollo Group Inc.	APOL
Apollo Investment Corp.	AINV
Apple Computer Inc.	AAPL
Applera Celera Group	CRA
Applied Industrial Techs. Inc.	AIT
Applied Mats. Inc.	AMAT
Applied Micro Circuits Corp.	AMCC
Approach Resources Inc.	AREX
Apricus Biosciences Inc.	APRI
AptarGroup Inc.	ATR
Aqua America Inc.	WTR
Arbitron Inc.	ARB
Arch Capital Group	ACGL
Arch Chemicals Inc.	ARJ

Arch Coal Inc.	ACI
Archer-Daniels-Midland Co.	ADM
Arcos Dorados Holdings Inc.	ARCO
Arctic Cat Inc.	ACAT
Ares Capital Corp.	ARCC
Argo Group International Holdings Ltd.	AGII
ARIAD Pharmaceuticals Inc.	ARIA
Ariba Inc.	ARBA
Arkansas Best Corp.	ABFS
ARM Holdings PLC	ARMH
ARMOUR Residential REIT Inc.	ARR
Armstrong World Indus. Inc.	AWI
ArQule Inc.	ARQL
Arris Group Inc.	ARRS
Arrow Electronics Inc.	ARW
ArthroCare Corp.	ARTC
Arthur J. Gallager & Co.	AJG
Artio Global Investors Inc.	ART
Aruba Networks Inc.	ARUN
ASA Ltd.	ASA
Asbury Automotive Group Inc	ABG
Ascena Retail Group Inc.	ASNA
Ashford Hospitality Trust Inc.	AHT
Ashland Inc.	ASH
Asianfo Hldgs. Inc.	ASIA
ASM International N.V.	ASMI
ASML Hldg. NV	ASML
Aspen Insurance Holdings Ltd.	AHL
Aspen Technology Inc.	AZPN
Asset Acceptance Capital Corp.	AACC

Associated Banc-Corp.	ASBC
Associated Estates Realty Corp.	AEC
Assurant Inc.	AIZ
Assured Guaranty Ltd.	AGO
Asta Funding Inc.	ASFI
Astec Industries Inc.	ASTE
Astoria Finan. Corp.	AF
AstraZeneca plc	AZN
AT&T Corp.	T
Athenahealth Inc.	ATHN
Atheros Comms. Inc.	ATHR
Atlantic Power Corp.	AT
Atlantic Tele-Network Inc.	ATNI
Atlas Air Worldwide Holdings Inc.	AAWW
Atlas Energy Inc.	ATLS
Atlas Pipeline Holdings LP	AHD
Atlas Pipeline Partners LP	APL
Atmel Corp.	ATML
ATMI Inc.	ATMI
Atmos Energy Corp.	ATO
ATP Oil & Gas Corp.	ATPG
Atwood Oceanics Inc.	ATW
AU Optronics Corp.	AUO
AudioCodes Ltd.	AUDC
Audiovox Corp.	VOXX
Aurizon Mines Ltd.	AZK
Autodesk Inc.	ADSK
Autoliv Inc.	ALV
Automatic Data Processing Inc.	ADP
AutoNation Inc.	AN

Autozone Inc.	AZO
Auxilium Pharmas. Inc.	AUXL
Avago Technologies Ltd.	AVGO
Avalon Rare Metals Inc.	AVL
Avalonbay Comm	AVB
Avatar Holdings Inc.	AVTR
AVEO Pharmaceuticals Inc.	AVEO
Avery Dennison Corp.	AVY
Avid Technology Inc.	AVID
Avis Budget Group Inc.	CAR
Avista Corp.	AVA
Avnet Inc.	AVT
Avon Products Inc.	AVP
AVX Corp.	AVX
AXA ADR	AXAHY
Axis Capital Hldgs. Ltd.	AXS
AXT Inc.	AXTI
AZZ Inc.	AZZ
B&G Foods Inc.	BGS
Badger Meter Inc.	BMI
Baidu.com Inc.	BIDU
Baker Hughes Inc.	BHI
Balchem Corp.	BCPC
Ball Corp.	BLL
Bally Techs. Inc.	BYI
Baltic Trading Limited	BALT
Banco Bilbao Vizcaya Argentaria SA ADR	BBVA
Banco Bradesco SA	BBD
Banco Santander Brasil S.A.	BSBR
Banco Santander SA	STD

Banco Santander-Chile	SAN
Bancolombia S.A.	CIB
BancorpSouth Inc.	BXS
Bank of America Corp.	BAC
Bank of Hawaii Corp.	BOH
Bank of Montreal	BMO
Bank of New York Co. Inc.	BK
Bank Of Nova Scotia (The)	BNS
Bank of the Ozarks Inc.	OZRK
BankUnited Inc.	BKU
Barclays iPath DJ-UBS Cotton TR Sub-Idx ETN	BAL
Barclays PLC	BCS
Barnes & Noble Inc.	BKS
Barnes Group Inc.	B
Barrick Gold Corp.	ABX
Basic Energy Services Inc.	BAS
Baxter Intl. Inc.	BAX
Baytex Energy Trust	BTE
BB&T Corp.	BBT
BCE Inc.	BCE
BE Aerospace Inc.	BEAV
Beacon Roofing Supply Inc.	BECN
Bebe Stores Inc.	BEBE
Beckman Coulter Inc.	BEC
Becton Dickinson & Co.	BDX
Bed Bath & Beyond Inc.	BBBY
Belden CDT Inc.	BDC
Belo Corp.	BLC
Bemis Co.	BMS
Benchmark Electronics Inc.	BHE

Berkshire Hathaway Inc. Class B	BRK.B
Berry Petroleum Co.	BRY
Best Buy Co. Inc.	BBY
BGC Partners Inc.	BGCP
BHP Billiton Ltd.	BHP
BHP Billiton PLC	BBL
Big 5 Sporting Goods Corp.	BGFV
Big Lots Inc.	BIG
Bill Barrett Corp.	BBG
Bio Reference Labs. Inc.	BRLI
Biogen Idec Inc.	BIIB
Biolase Technology Inc.	BLTI
BioMarin Pharma. Inc.	BMRN
BioMed Realty Trust Inc.	BMR
BioMimetic Therapeutics Inc.	BMTI
Bio-Rad Lab. Inc. Class A	BIO
Biotech HOLDRs Trust	BBH
Biotechnology SPDR	XBI
BioTime Inc.	BTX
Bitauto Holdings Ltd.	BITA
BJs Restaurants Inc.	BJRI
BJs Wholesale Club Inc.	BJ
Black Box Corp.	BBOX
Black Hills Corp.	BKH
Blackbaud Inc.	BLKB
Blackboard Inc.	BBBB
BlackRock Inc.	BLK
BlackRock Kelso Capital Corp.	BKCC
Blackrock World Investment Trust	BWC
Blackstone Group LP (The)	BX

BLDRS Emerging Markets 50 ADR	ADRE
Blount Intl. Inc.	BLT
Blue Coat Systems Inc.	BCSI
Blue Nile Inc.	NILE
Blyth Inc.	BTH
BMC Software Inc.	BMC
Boardwalk Pipeline Partners LP	BWP
Bob Evans Farms Inc.	BOBE
Boeing Co.	BA
Boise Inc.	BZ
BOK Financial Corp.	BOKF
Bona Film Group Limited	BONA
Bon-Ton Stores Inc.	BONT
Booz Allen Hamilton Inc.	BAH
BorgWarner Inc.	BWA
Boston Beer Co. Inc.	SAM
Boston Private Fin. Hldgs. Inc.	BPFH
Boston Properties Inc.	BXP
Boston Scientific Corp.	BSX
Bottomline Technologies Inc.	EPAY
Boyd Gaming Corp.	BYD
BP Prudhoe Bay Royalty Trust	BPT
Brady Corp.	BRC
Brandywine Realty Trust	BDN
Brasil Telecom SA	BTM
Braskem S.A.	BAK
Bravo Brio Restaurant Group Inc.	BBRG
BRE Properties Inc	BRE
Breitburn Energy Partners LP	BBEP
BRF - Brasil Foods S.A.	BRFS

Bridgepoint Education Inc.	BPI
Briggs & Stratton Corp	BGG
Brigham Exploration Co.	BEXP
Brightpoint Inc.	CELL
Brinker Intl. Inc.	EAT
Brinks Co.	BCO
Bristol-Myers Squibb Co.	BMY
Bristow Group Inc.	BRS
British American Tobacco plc	BTI
British Petroleum Co.	BP
Broadband HOLDRs	BDH
Broadcom Corp.	BRCM
Broadridge Financial Solutions Inc.	BR
BroadSoft Inc.	BSFT
Brocade Comm. Systems Inc.	BRCD
Bronco Drilling Co. Inc.	BRNC
Brookdale Senior Living Inc.	BKD
Brookfield Asset Management Inc.	BAM
Brookfield Infrastructure Partners LP	BIP
Brookfield Properties Corp.	BPO
Brookline Bancorp Inc.	BRKL
Brooks Automation Inc.	BRKS
Brown & Brown Inc.	BRO
Brown Shoe Co. Inc.	BWS
Brown-Forman Corp. Class B	BF.B
Bruker BioSciences Corp.	BRKR
Brunswick Corp.	BC
BSQUARE Corp.	BSQR
Buckeye Partners LP	BPL
Buckeye Techs. Inc.	BKI

Buckle Inc.	BKE
Bucyrus Intl. Inc.	BUCY
Buffalo Wild Wings Inc.	BWLD
Build-A-Bear Workshop Inc.	BBW
Bunge Ltd.	BG
C.R. Bard Inc.	BCR
Cabelas Inc.	CAB
Cablevision Sys. Corp. Class A	CVC
Cabot Corp.	CBT
Cabot Microelectronics	CCMP
Cabot Oil & Gas Corp.	COG
Cache Inc.	CACH
CACI Intl. Inc.	CACI
Cadence Design Systems Inc.	CDNS
Cadence Pharmaceuticals Inc.	CADX
Cadiz Inc.	CDZI
Cal Dive International Inc	DVR
Calamos Asset Management Inc.	CLMS
Calgon Carbon Corp.	CCC
Cali Realty Corp	CLI
California Pizza Kitchen	CPKI
California Water Service Group	CWT
Caliper Life Sciences Inc.	CALP
Calix Inc.	CALX
Callaway Golf Co.	ELY
Callidus Software Inc.	CALD
Callon Petroleum Co.	CPE
Cal-Maine Foods Inc.	CALM
Calpine Corp.	CPN
Calumet Specialty Products Partners LP	CLMT

Camden Property Trust	CPT
Cameco Corp.	CCJ
Camelot Information Systems Inc.	CIS
Campbell Soup Co.	CPB
Campus Crest Communities Inc.	CCG
Canadian Imperial Bank of Commerce	CM
Canadian National Railway Co.	CNI
Canadian Natural Res. Ltd.	CNQ
Canadian Pacific Railway Ltd.	CP
Canadian Solar Inc.	CSIQ
Canon Inc.	CAJ
Cantel Medical Corp.	CMN
Capella Education Co.	CPLA
Capital One Financial Corp.	COF
Capital Product Partners LP	CPLP
Capital Senior Living Corp.	CSU
CapitalSource Inc.	CSE
Capitol Federal Financial	CFFN
Capstead Mortgage Corp.	CMO
Carbo Ceramics Inc.	CRR
Cardinal Health Inc.	CAH
Cardiome Pharma Corp.	CRME
Cardtronics Inc.	CATM
Career Education Corp.	CECO
Carefusion Corp.	CFN
Caribou Coffee Company Inc.	CBOU
Carlisle Companies Inc.	CSL
Carmax Inc.	KMX
Carmike Cinemas Inc.	CKEC
Carnival Corp.	CCL

Carnival PLC	CUK
Carpenter Tech. Corp.	CRS
Carrizo Oil & Gas Inc.	CRZO
Carter`s Inc.	CRI
Casella Waste Sys. Inc.	CWST
Caseys General Stores Inc.	CASY
Cash America Intl. Inc.	CSH
Catalyst Health Solutions Inc.	CHSI
Caterpillar Inc.	CAT
Cathay General Bancorp	CATY
Cato Corp.	CATO
Cavium Networks Inc.	CAVM
CB Richard Ellis Group Inc.	CBG
Cbeyond Inc.	CBEY
CBIZ Inc.	CBZ
CBL & Associates Properties Inc.	CBL
CBOE Holdings Inc.	CBOE
CBS Corp. Class A	CBS.A
CBS Corp. Class B	CBS
CDI Corp.	CDI
CEC Entertainment Inc.	CEC
Cedar Fair LP	FUN
Cedar Shopping Centers Inc. REIT	CDR
Celadon Group Inc.	CGI
Celanese Corp.	CE
Celestica Inc.	CLS
Celgene Corp.	CELG
Cellcom Israel Ltd.	CEL
Cemex SA de CV	CX
Cenovus Energy Inc.	CVE

Centene Corp.	CNC
CenterPoint Energy Inc.	CNP
Centrais Electricas Brasileiras SA	EBR
Centrais Electricas Brasileiras SA Class B	EBR.B
Central European Dist. Corp.	CEDC
Central European Media Ents. Ltd.	CETV
Central Garden & Pet Co.	CENT
Central Garden & Pet Co.	CENTA
Central Pacific Financial Corp.	CPF
Century Aluminum Co.	CENX
CenturyTel Inc.	CTL
Cenveo Inc.	CVO
Cephalon Inc.	CEPH
Cepheid	CPHD
Ceradyne Inc.	CRDN
Ceragon Networks Ltd.	CRNT
Cerner Corp.	CERN
CEVA Inc.	CEVA
CF Industries Hldgs. Inc.	CF
CGI Group Inc.	GIB
CH Robinson Worldwide Inc.	CHRW
Changyou.com Ltd.	CYOU
Charles River Lab	CRL
Charles Schwab Inc.	SCHW
Chart Indus. Inc.	GTLS
Check Point Software Techs. Ltd.	CHKP
Checkpoint Systems Inc.	CKP
Cheesecake Factory Inc.	CAKE
Chemed Corp.	CHE
Chemical & Mining Co. of Chile Inc.	SQM

Chemical Financial Corp.	CHFC
Chemtura Corp.	CHMT
Cheniere Energy Inc.	LNG
Cheniere Energy Partners	CQP
Chesapeake Energy Corp.	CHK
Chesapeake Midstream Partners LP	CHKM
ChevronTexaco	CVX
Chicago Bridge & Iron Co NV	CBI
Chicago Merc. Exch. Hldgs. Inc.	CME
Chicos FAS Inc.	CHS
Childrens Place Retail Stores	PLCE
China Automotive Systems Inc.	CAAS
China Digital TV Holding Co. Ltd.	STV
China Finance Online Co. Ltd.	JRJC
China Fire & Security Group Inc.	CFSG
China Green Agriculture Inc.	CGA
China Life Insurance Co. Ltd.	LFC
China Lodging Group Limited	HTHT
China Medical Techs. Inc.	CMED
China Ming Yang Wind Power Group Ltd.	MY
China Natural Gas Inc.	CHNG
China New Borun Corp.	BORN
China Real Estate Information Corp.	CRIC
China Security & Surveillance Tech. Inc.	CSR
China Southern Airlines Co. Ltd.	ZNH
China Techfaith Wireless Comm. Tech. Ltd.	CNTF
China Telecom Corp. Ltd.	CHA
China Telecom Limited ADR	CHL
China Unicom Ltd.	CHU
China Yuchai Intl. Ltd.	CYD

China-Biotics Inc.	CHBT
ChinaCast Education Corp.	CAST
Chipotle Mexican Grill Inc.	CMG
Chiquita Brands Intl. Inc.	CQB
Choice Hotels Intl. Inc.	CHH
Christopher & Banks Corp.	CBK
Chubb Corp.	CB
Chunghwa Telecom Co. Ltd.	CHT
Church & Dwight Co. Inc.	CHD
Churchill Downs Inc.	CHDN
CIBER Inc.	CBR
Ciena Corp.	CIEN
CIGNA Corp.	CI
Cimarex Energy Co.	XEC
Cincinnati Financial Corp.	CINF
Cinemark Holdings Inc.	CNK
Cintas Corp.	CTAS
CIRCOR International Inc.	CIR
Cirrus Logic Inc.	CRUS
Cisco Systems Inc.	CSCO
CIT Group Inc.	CIT
Citi Trends	CTRN
Citizens Inc.	CIA
Citrix Systems Inc.	CTXS
City Holding Co.	CHCO
City National Corp.	CYN
City Telecom HK Ltd.	CTEL
CLARCOR Inc.	CLC
Claymore China Technology	CQQQ
Claymore/AlphaShares China Real Estate	TAO

Claymore/AlphaShares China Small Cap	HAO
Claymore/BNY BRIC ADR	EEB
Claymore/MAC Global Solar Energy	TAN
Claymore/NYSE Arca Airline	FAA
Clean Energy Fuels Corp.	CLNE
Clean Harbor Inc	CLH
Clear Channel Outdoor Hldgs. Inc.	CCO
Clearwater Paper Corp.	CLW
Clearwire Corp.	CLWR
Cleco Corp.	CNL
Cleveland Biolabs Inc.	CBLI
Cleveland-Cliffs Inc.	CLF
ClickSoftware Technologies Ltd.	CKSW
Clorox Co.	CLX
Cloud Peak Energy Inc.	CLD
CMS Energy Corp.	CMS
CNA Financial Corp.	CNA
CNH Global NV	CNH
Cninsure Inc.	CISG
CNOOC Ltd.	CEO
Coach Inc.	COH
Cobalt International Energy Inc.	CIE
Coca-Cola Co.	KO
Coca-Cola Enterprises Inc.	CCE
Coca-Cola FEMSA S.A.B de CV	KOF
Coeur d`Alene Mines Corp.	CDE
Cogdell Spencer Inc.	CSA
Cogent Communications Group Inc.	CCOI
Cognex Corp.	CGNX
Cognizant Tech. Solution Corp.	CTSH

Cohen & Steers Inc.	CNS
Coherent Inc.	COHR
Cohu Inc.	COHU
Coinstar Inc.	CSTR
Colfax Corp.	CFX
Colgate-Palmolive Co.	CL
Colonial Properties Trust REIT	CLP
Colony Financial Inc.	CLNY
Columbia Banking System Inc.	COLB
Columbia Sportswear Corp.	COLM
Columbus Mckinnon Corp.	CMCO
Comcast Corp.	CMCSK
Comcast Corp. Class A	CMCSA
Comerica Inc.	CMA
Comfort Systems USA Inc.	FIX
Commerce Bancshares Inc.	CBSH
Commercial Metals Co.	CMC
Commercial Vehicle Group Inc.	CVGI
Commonwealth REIT	CWH
Community Bank System Inc.	CBU
Community Health Systems Inc.	CYH
CommVault Systems Inc.	CVLT
Compagnie G G-Veritas	CGV
Companhia Brasileira de Distribuicao	CBD
Companhia de Bebidas das Americas	ABV
Companhia de Saneamento Basico do Estado de Sao Pa	SBS
Companhia Energetica de Minas Gerais ADS	CIG
Companhia Paranaense de Energia	ELP
Companhia Siderurgica Nacional	SID
Companhia Vale ADS	VALE

Compania de Minas Buenaventura SA	BVN
Compass Diversified Holdings	CODI
Compass Minerals Intl. Inc.	CMP
Complete Production Services Inc.	CPX
Computer Associates Intl. Inc.	CA
Computer Programs & Systems Inc.	CPSI
Computer Sciences Corp.	CSC
Compuware Corp.	CPWR
comScore Inc.	SCOR
Comstock Resources Inc.	CRK
Comtech Group Inc.	COGO
Comtech Telecom. Corp.	CMTL
ConAgra Inc.	CAG
Conceptus Inc.	CPTS
Concho Resources Inc.	CXO
Concur Techs. Inc.	CNQR
CONMED Corp.	CNMD
Conns Inc.	CONN
ConocoPhillips	COP
Conseco Inc.	CNO
Consol Energy Inc.	CNX
Consolidated Comms. Hldgs. Inc.	CNSL
Consolidated Edison Inc.	ED
Consolidated Graphics Inc.	CGX
Constant Contact Inc.	CTCT
Constellation Brands Inc.	STZ
Constellation Energy Grp	CEG
Consumer Discretionary SPDR	XLY
Consumer Staples Select Sector SPDR	XLP
Contango Oil & Gas Co.	MCF

Continental Resources Inc.	CLR
Continucare Corp.	CNU
Convergys Corp	CVG
Con-Way Inc.	CNW
Cooper Cameron Corp.	CAM
Cooper Companies Inc.	COO
Cooper Industries Inc.	CBE
Cooper Tire & Rubber Co.	CTB
Copa Holdings SA	CPA
Copano Energy LLC	CPNO
Copart Inc.	CPRT
Core Labs. NV	CLB
CoreLogic Inc.	CLGX
Corn Products International	CPO
Corning Inc.	GLW
Corporate Executive Board Co.	EXBD
Corporate Office Properties Trust Inc. REIT	OFC
Corrections Corp. of America	CXW
Cosan Ltd. Class A	CZZ
Cost Plus Inc.	CPWM
Costamare Inc.	CMRE
CoStar Group Inc.	CSGP
Costco Companies Inc.	COST
Cott Corp.	COT
Cousins Properties Inc.	CUZ
Covance Inc.	CVD
Covanta Holding Corp.	CVA
Coventry Health Care Inc.	CVH
Covidien Ltd.	COV
CPFL Energia SA	CPL

Cracker Barrel Old Country Stores Inc.	CBRL
Craft Brewers Alliance Inc.	HOOK
Crane Co.	CR
Cray Inc.	CRAY
Credicorp Ltd.	BAP
Credit Suisse Cushing 30 MLP ETN	MLPN
Credit Suisse Group	CS
Cree Research Inc.	CREE
CRH plc	CRH
Crocs Inc.	CROX
Cross Country Inc.	CCRN
Crosstex Energy Inc.	XTXI
Crosstex Energy LP	XTEX
Crown Castle Intl. Corp.	CCI
Crown Holdings Inc.	CCK
Crucell NV	CRXLY
Crude Carriers Corp.	CRU
CryoLife Inc.	CRY
CSG Systems Intl. Inc.	CSGS
CSX Corp.	CSX
CTC Media Inc.	CTCM
Ctrip.com Intl. Ltd.	CTRP
CTS Corp.	CTS
Cubic Corp.	CUB
Cubist Pharmas. Inc.	CBST
Cullen/Frost Bankers Inc.	CFR
Cumberland Pharmaceuticals Inc.	CPIX
Cummins Engine Co. Inc.	CMI
CurrencyShares Australian Dollar	FXA
CurrencyShares British Pound Sterling	FXB

CurrencyShares Canadian Dollar	FXC
CurrencyShares Euro	FXE
CurrencyShares Japanese Yen	FXY
CurrencyShares Mexican Peso	FXM
CurrencyShares Swedish Krona	FXS
CurrencyShares Swiss Franc	FXF
Curtiss-Wright Corp.	CW
Cutera Inc.	CUTR
CVB Financial Corp.	CVBF
CVR Energy Inc.	CVI
CVR Partners LP	UAN
CVS Corp.	CVS
Cyberonics Inc.	CYBX
Cymer Inc.	CYMI
Cynosure Inc.	CYNO
Cypress Semiconductor Corp.	CY
Cypress Sharpridge	CYS
Cytec Industries Inc.	CYT
Cytori Therapeutics Inc.	CYTX
D.R. Horton Inc.	DHI
Daimlerchrysler AG	DDAIF
Daktronics Inc.	DAKT
Dana Holding Corp.	DAN
Danaher Corp.	DHR
Danvers Bancorp Inc.	DNBK
Darden Restaurants Inc.	DRI
Darling Intl. Inc.	DAR
Datalink Corp.	DTLK
DaVita Inc.	DVA
Dawson Geophysical Co.	DWSN

DCP Midstream Partners LP	DPM
DCT Industrial Trust Inc.	DCT
DDI Corp.	DDIC
DealerTrack Holdings Inc.	TRAK
Dean Foods Co.	DF
Deckers Outdoor Corp.	DECK
Deer Consumer Products Inc.	DEER
Deere & Co.	DE
Delcath Systems Inc.	DCTH
Delek US Holdings Inc.	DK
Dell Computer Corp.	DELL
Delphi Financial Group Inc.	DFG
Delta Air Lines Inc.	DAL
Deluxe Corp.	DLX
Demand Media Inc.	DMD
DemandTec Inc.	DMAN
Denbury Resources Inc.	DNR
Dendreon Corp.	DNDN
DentsPly Intl. Inc.	XRAY
Depomed Inc.	DEPO
Destination Maternity Corp.	DEST
Deutsche Bank AG	DB
Deutsche Telekom AG ADR	DTEGY
Developers Diversified Realty Corp.	DDR
Devon Energy Corp.	DVN
DeVRY Inc.	DV
DexCom Inc.	DXCM
DG FastChannel Inc.	DGIT
Diageo PLC	DEO
Diamond Foods Inc.	DMND

Diamond Offshore Drilling Inc.	DO
Diamondrock Hospitality Co.	DRH
DIAMONDS HOLDRs Trust	DIA
Diana Shipping Inc.	DSX
Dice Holdings Inc.	DHX
Dicks Sporting Goods Inc.	DKS
Diebold Inc.	DBD
Digital Realty Trust Inc.	DLR
Digital River Inc.	DRIV
DigitalGlobe Inc.	DGI
Dillards Inc.	DDS
Dime Community Bancshares Inc.	DCOM
DineEquity Inc.	DIN
Diodes Inc.	DIOD
Directv Group Inc. (The)	DTV
Direxion Daily 10 Yr Trsy BEAR 3X Shares	TYO
Direxion Daily 10 Yr Trsy BULL 3X Shares	TYD
Direxion Daily 30 Yr Trsy BEAR 3X Shares	TMV
Direxion Daily 30 Yr Trsy BULL 3X Shares	TMF
Direxion Daily China Select ADR Bear 3X	CZI
Direxion Daily China Select ADR Bull 3X	CZM
Direxion Daily Devlpd Mrkts BEAR 3X	DPK
Direxion Daily Devlpd Mrkts BULL 3X Shares	DZK
Direxion Daily Gold Miners Bull 2x	NUGT
Direxion Daily Latin America Bear 3X	LHB
Direxion Daily Latin America Bull 3X	LBJ
Direxion Daily Natural Gas Related Bear 2x	FCGS
Direxion Daily Natural Gas Related Bull 2x	FCGL
Direxion Daily Real Estate 3X BULL	DRN
Direxion Daily Real Estate BEAR 3X	DRV

Direxion Daily Semicondctor BEAR 3X	SOXS
Direxion Daily Semicondctor BULL 3X	SOXL
Direxion Emerging Markets BEAR 3X	EDZ
Direxion Emerging Markets BULL 3X	EDC
Direxion Gold Miners Bear 2x	DUST
Direxion Mid Cap BEAR 3X	MWN
Direxion Mid Cap BULL 3X	MWJ
Direxion Shares Energy BEAR 3x	ERY
Direxion Shares Energy BULL 3x	ERX
Direxion Shares Financial BEAR 3x	FAZ
Direxion Shares Financial BULL 3x	FAS
Direxion Shares Large Cap BEAR 3x	BGZ
Direxion Shares Large Cap BULL 3x	BGU
Direxion Shares Small Cap BEAR 3x	TZA
Direxion Shares Small Cap BULL 3x	TNA
Direxion Technology BEAR 3X Shares	TYP
Direxion Technology BULL 3X Shares	TYH
Discover Financial Services	DFS
Discovery Comms. Inc.	DISCA
Discovery Communications Inc.	DISCK
Disney (The Walt) Co.	DIS
DJ Euro STOXX 50	FEZ
Dolan Media Company	DM
Dolby Laboratories Inc.	DLB
Dole Food Company Inc.	DOLE
Dollar Financial Corp.	DLLR
Dollar General Corp.	DG
Dollar Thrifty Automotive Group Inc.	DTG
Dollar Tree Stores Inc.	DLTR
Dominion Resources Inc.	D

Dominos Pizza Inc.	DPZ
Domtar Corp.	UFS
Donaldson Co. Inc.	DCI
Dorchester Minerals LP	DMLP
Double Eagle Petroleum Co.	DBLE
Douglas Emmett Inc.	DEI
Dover Corp.	DOV
Dow Chemical Co.	DOW
DPL Inc.	DPL
Dr Pepper Snapple Group Inc.	DPS
DragonWave Inc.	DRWI
DreamWorks Animation SKG Inc.	DWA
Dresser-Rand Group Inc.	DRC
Dril-Quip Inc.	DRQ
DSP Group Inc.	DSPG
DST Systems Inc.	DST
DSW Inc.	DSW
DTE Energy Co. Hldgs.	DTE
du Pont (E.I.) de Nemours & Co.	DD
Ducommun Inc.	DCO
Duff & Phelps Corp.	DUF
Duke Power Co.	DUK
Duke Realty Investment Inc.	DRE
Dun & Bradstreet Corp.	DNB
Duncan Energy Partners LP	DEP
DuPont Fabros Technology Inc.	DFT
DXP Enterprises Inc.	DXPE
Dycom Indus. Inc.	DY
Dynamic Materials Corp.	BOOM
Dynavox Inc.	DVOX

Dynegy Inc.	DYN
Dynex Capital Inc.	DX
E*TRADE Financial Corp.	C
E.W. Scripps Co. Class A	SSP
Eagle Materials Inc.	EXP
Eagle Rock Energy Partners L.P.	EROC
Earthlink Inc.	ELNK
East West Bancorp Inc.	EWBC
EastGroup Properties Inc.	EGP
Eastman Chemical Co.	EMN
Eaton Corp.	ETN
Eaton Vance Corp.	EV
eBay Inc.	EBAY
Ebix Inc.	EBIX
Echelon Corp.	ELON
Echo Global Logistics Inc.	ECHO
EchoStar Comm. Corp.	DISH
Echostar Holding Corp.	SATS
ECOLAB Inc.	ECL
E-Commerce China Dangdang Inc.	DANG
Ecopetrol SA	EC
Edison Intl.	EIX
Education Management Corp.	EDMC
Education Realty Trust Inc.	EDR
Edwards LifeSciences	EW
eHealth Inc.	EHTH
E-House (China) Holdings Ltd.	EJ
El Paso Corp.	EP
El Paso Electric Co.	EE
El Paso Pipeline Partners LP	EPB

Elan Corp.	ELN
Elbit Systems	ESLT
Eldorado Gold Corp.	EGO
Electro Scientific Ind	ESIO
Electronic Arts Inc.	ERTS
Electronics For Imaging Inc.	EFII
Elements MLCX Grains ETN	GRU
eLong Inc.	LONG
eMagin Corp.	EMAN
Embraer Aircraft ADR	ERJ
EMC Corp.	EMC
EMCOR Group Inc.	EME
Emdeon Inc.	EM
Emergency Medical Services Corp.	EMS
Emergent BioSolutions Inc.	EBS
Emeritus Corp.	ESC
Emerson Electric Co.	EMR
Empire District Electric Co.	EDE
EMS Technologies Inc.	ELMG
Emulex Corp.	ELX
Enbridge Energy Management LLC	EEQ
Enbridge Energy Partners LP	EEP
Enbridge Inc.	ENB
EnCana Corp.	ECA
Encore Capital Group Inc.	ECPG
Encore Energy Partners LP	ENP
Encore Wire Corp.	WIRE
Endeavour International Corp.	END
Endeavour Silver Corp.	EXK
Endo Pharma. Hld.	ENDP

Endologix Inc.	ELGX
Endurance Specialty Hldgs. Ltd.	ENH
Energen Corp.	EGN
Energizer Hldgs. Inc.	ENR
Energy Partners Ltd.	EPL
Energy Sector SPDR	XLE
Energy Transfer Equity L.P.	ETE
Energy Transfer Partners LP	ETP
Energy XXI (Bermuda) Limited	EXXI
EnergySolutions Inc.	ES
EnerNOC Inc.	ENOC
Enerplus Resources Fund	ERF
Enersis SA ADR	ENI
EnerSys	ENS
Eni SpA ADS	E
EnPro Industries Inc.	NPO
ENSCO Intl. Inc.	ESV
Ensign Group Inc. (The)	ENSG
Entegris Inc.	ENTG
Entercom Communications Corp.	ETM
Entergy Corp.	ETR
Enterprise Products Partners LP	EPD
Entertainment Properties Trust	EPR
Entropic Communications Inc.	ENTR
Enzon Inc.	ENZN
EOG Resources Group	EOG
Epicor Software Corp.	EPIC
EPIQ Systems Inc.	EPIQ
Equifax Inc.	EFX
Equinix Inc.	EQIX

Equitable Resources Inc.	EQT
Equity Lifestyles Properties Inc.	ELS
Equity One Inc. REIT	EQY
Equity Residential Properties Trust	EQR
eResearch Technology Inc.	ERT
ESCO Techs. Inc.	ESE
Essex Property Trust Inc.	ESS
Estee Lauder Co. Inc. Class A	EL
Esterline Tech. Corp.	ESL
Ethan Allen Interiors Inc.	ETH
Euronet Worldwide Inc.	EEFT
EV Energy Partners LP	EVEP
Evercore Partners Inc.	EVR
Evolution Petroleum Corp.	EPM
Exact Sciences Corp.	EXAS
Exar Corp.	EXAR
Excel Trust Inc.	EXL
EXCO Resources Inc.	XCO
Exelixis Inc.	EXEL
Exelon Corp.	EXC
Exeter Resource Corp.	XRA
Exide Techs.	XIDE
Expedia Inc.	EXPE
Expeditors Intern. Wa. Inc.	EXPD
Express Inc.	EXPR
Express Scripts Inc. Class A	ESRX
Exterran Hldgs.	EXH
Extorre Gold Mines Ltd.	XG
Extra Space Storage Inc.	EXR
Exxon Mobil Corp.	XOM

EZchip Semiconductor Ltd.	EZCH
Ezcorp Inc.	EZPW
F.N.B. Corp.	FNB
F5 Networks Inc.	FFIV
FactorShares 2X Crude Oil Bull / S&P 500 Bear	FOL
FactorShares 2X Gold Bull / S&P 500 Bear	FSG
FactorShares 2X S&P 500 Bull / TBond Bear	FSE
FactorShares 2X S&P 500 Bull / USD Bear	FSU
FactorShares 2X TBond Bull / S&P 500 Bear	FSA
Factset Research Sys. Inc.	FDS
Fair Isaac Corp.	FICO
Fairchild Semi. Inter. Inc.	FCS
Fairfax Fin. Hldgs. Ltd.	FRFHF
Family Dollar Stores Inc.	FDO
Famous Daves of America Inc.	DAVE
FARO Techs. Inc.	FARO
Fastenal Co.	FAST
Federal Agricultural Mortgage Corp.	AGM
Federal Express Corp.	FDX
Federal Realty Investment Trust	FRT
Federal Signal Corp.	FSS
Federal-Mogul Corp.	FDML
Federated Investors Inc.	FII
FEI Co.	FEIC
FelCor Lodging Trust Inc.	FCH
Ferrellgas Partners LP	FGP
Ferro Corp.	FOE
Fibria Celulose SA	FBR
Fidelity National Financial Inc.	FNF
Fidelity National Information Services Inc.	FIS

Fifth Street Finance Corp.	FSC
Fifth Third Bancorp.	FITB
Financial Engines Inc.	FNGN
Financial Sector SPDR	XLF
Finisar Corp.	FNSR
Finish Line (The) Class A	FINL
First American Fin. Corp. (The)	FAF
First Busey Corp.	BUSE
First Cash Financial Services Inc.	FCFS
First Commonwealth Financial Corp.	FCF
First Community Bancshares Inc.	FCBC
First Financial Bancorp.	FFBC
First Financial Northwest Inc.	FFNW
First Horizon National Corp.	FHN
First Industrial Realty Trust Inc.	FR
First Majestic Silver Corp.	AG
First Midwest Bancorp Inc.	FMBI
First Niagara Fin. Group Inc.	FNFG
First Potomac Realty Trust REIT	FPO
First Republic Bank	FRC
First Solar Inc.	FSLR
First Trust Dow Jones Select MicroCap	FDM
First Trust ISE - Revere Natural Gas	FCG
First Trust ISE Chindia	FNI
First Trust ISE Global Copper	CU
First Trust ISE Global Platinum	PLTM
First Trust ISE Global Wind Energy	FAN
First Trust ISE Water	FIW
Firstenergy Corp.	FE
FirstMerit Corp.	FMER

FirstTrust Dow Jones Internet	FDN
FirstTrust Financials AlphaDEX	FXO
FirstTrust NYSE Arca Biotech	FBT
Five Star Quality Care Inc.	FVE
Flamel Techs. SA ADS	FLML
FleetCor Technologies Inc.	FLT
Flextronics Intl. Ltd.	FLEX
Flir Systems Inc.	FLIR
Flotek Indus. Inc.	FTK
Flowers Foods	FLO
Flowserve Corp.	FLS
Flserv Inc.	FISV
Fluor Corp.	FLR
FMC Corp.	FMC
FMC Techs. Inc.	FTI
Focus Media Holding Ltd.	FMCN
Fomento Economico Mexicano SA de CV	FMX
Foot Locker Inc.	FL
Ford Motor Co.	F
Forest City Enterprises Inc. Class A	FCE.A
Forest Labs.	FRX
Forest Oil Corp.	FST
Forestar Real Estate Group Inc.	FOR
FormFactor Inc.	FORM
Fortinet Inc.	FTNT
Fortress Investment Group LLC	FIG
Fortune Brands Inc.	FO
Forward Air Corp.	FWRD
Fossil Inc.	FOSL
Foster Wheeler Ltd.	FWLT

France Telecom SA ADR	FTE
Franklin Electric Co. Inc.	FELE
Franklin Resources Inc.	BEN
Franklin Street Properties Corp.	FSP
Freds Inc.	FRED
Freeport-McMoran Copper & Gold Inc.	FCX
Fresenius Medical Services ADS	FMS
Fresh Del Monte Prod. Inc.	FDP
Fresh Market Inc. (The)	TFM
Frontier Comms. Corp.	FTR
Frontier Oil Corp.	FTO
Frontline Ltd.	FRO
FTI Consulting Inc.	FCN
Fuel Systems Solutions Inc.	FSYS
Fuel Tech NV	FTEK
Fulton Financial Corp.	FULT
Furiex Pharmaceuticals Inc.	FURX
Fushi Copperweld Inc.	FSIN
FX Energy Inc.	FXEN
FXCM Inc.	FXCM
Gafisa SA	GFA
Gamestop Corp.	GME
Gammon Lake Resources Inc.	GRS
Gannett Co. Inc	GCI
Gap Inc.	GPS
Gardner Denver Inc.	GDI
Garmin Ltd.	GRMN
Gartner Inc.	IT
GATX Corp.	GMT
Gaylord Entertainment Co.	GET

Gen Probe Inc.	GPRO
Genco Shipping & Trading Ltd.	GNK
Gencorp Inc.	GY
General Cable Corp.	BGC
General Communication Inc.	GNCMA
General Dynamics Corp.	GD
General Electric Co.	GE
General Growth Properties Inc.	GGP
General Mills Inc.	GIS
General Motors Corp.	GM
Genesco Inc.	GCO
Genesee & Wyoming Inc.	GWR
Genesis Energy LP	GEL
Genomic Health Inc.	GHDX
Genpact Ltd.	G
Gentex Corp.	GNTX
Gentiva Health Services Inc.	GTIV
Genuine Parts Co.	GPC
Genworth Financial Inc.	GNW
Geo Group Inc.	GEO
GeoEye Inc.	GEOY
Geokinetics Inc.	GOK
GeoResources Inc.	GEOI
Georgia Gulf Corp.	GGC
Gerber Scientific Inc.	GRB
Gerdau SA	GGB
Getty Realty Corp.	GTY
Giant Interactive Group Inc.	GA
G-III Apparel Group Ltd.	GIII
Gildan Activewear Inc.	GIL

Gilead Sciences Inc.	GILD
Given Imaging Ltd.	GIVN
Glacier Bancorp Inc.	GBCI
Gladstone Capital Corp.	GLAD
GlaxoSmithKline PLC	GSK
Glimcher Realty Trust	GRT
Global China X Financials	CHIX
Global Crossing Ltd.	GLBC
Global Industries Ltd.	GLBL
Global Partners LP	GLP
Global Payments Inc.	GPN
Global Power Equipment Group Inc.	GLPW
Global X China Consumer	CHIQ
Global X China Industrials	CHII
Global X China Tech.	CHIB
Global X Copper Miners	COPX
Global X Silver Miners	SIL
Global X Uranium	URA
GlobalX Gold Explorers	GLDX
GlobalX Solactive Global Lithium	LIT
Globe Specialty Metals Inc.	GSM
GMX Resources Inc.	GMXR
GNC Corp.	GNC
Gol Linhas Aereas Inteligentes	GOL
Golar LNG Ltd.	GLNG
Golar LNG Partners LP	GMLP
Gold Fields Ltd.	GFI
Gold Resource Corp.	GORO
Goldcorp Inc.	GG
Golden Minerals Company	AUMN

Goldman Sachs Group	GS
Golub Capital BDC Inc.	GBDC
Goodrich Corp.	GR
Goodrich Petroleum Corp.	GDP
Goodyear Tire & Rubber Co.	GT
Google Inc.	GOOG
Government Properties Income Trust	GOV
Graco Inc.	GGG
Graftech Intl. Ltd.	GTI
Graham Corp.	GHM
Graham Packaging Co Inc.	GRM
Grainger (W.W.) Inc.	GWW
Gran Tierra Energy Inc.	GTE
Grand Canyon Education Inc.	LOPE
Granite Construction Inc	GVA
Graphic Packaging Holding Company	GPK
Great Lakes Dredge & Dock Corp.	GLDD
Great Plains Energy Inc.	GXP
Green Dot Corp.	GDOT
Green Mountain Coffee Roasters Inc.	GMCR
Green Plains Renewable Energy Inc.	GPRE
Greenbrier Companies Inc. (The)	GBX
GreenHaven Continuous Commodity	GCC
Greenhill & Co Inc.	GHL
Greenlight Capital Reinsurance Ltd.	GLRE
Greif Inc.	GEF
Griffon Corp.	GFF
Group I Automotive Inc.	GPI
Grupo Aeroportuario Centro Norte S.A. de C.V.	OMAB
Grupo Aeroportuario del Pacifico S.A. de C.V.	PAC

Grupo Aeroportuario Del Sureste SA de CV	ASR
Grupo Simec S.A. de C.V.	SIM
Grupo Televisa S.A. ADR	TV
GSI Commerce Inc.	GSIC
GSI Group Inc.	GSIG
GSI Technology Inc.	GSIT
GT Solar Intl. Inc.	SOLR
GTx Inc.	GTXI
Guangshen Railway Co. Ltd.	GSH
Guess Inc.	GES
Gulf Island Fabrication Inc.	GIFI
Gulfmark Offshore Inc.	GLF
Gulfport Energy Corp.	GPOR
H&E Equipment Srvs. Inc.	HEES
H&R Block Inc.	HRB
Haemonetics Corp.	HAE
Hain Food Group Inc	HAIN
Halliburton Co.	HAL
Halo Technology Holdings Inc.	HALO
Hancock Holding Co.	HBHC
HanesBrands Inc.	HBI
Hanger Orthopedic Group Inc.	HGR
Hanover Insurance Group Inc.	THG
Hansen Natural Corp.	HANS
Harbin Electric Inc.	HRBN
Harley-Davidson Inc.	HOG
Harman Intl. Indus. Inc.	HAR
Harmonic Lightwaves Inc.	HLIT
Harmony Gold Mining Co. Ltd.	HMY
Harris Corp.	HRS

Harry Winston Diamond Corp.	HWD
Harsco Corp.	HSC
Harte-Hanks Inc.	HHS
Hartford Fin. Srvs. Group Inc.	HIG
Hartland Express	HTLD
Harvest Natural Resources Inc.	HNR
Hasbro Inc.	HAS
Hatteras Financial Corp.	HTS
Hawaiian Electric Indus. Inc.	HE
Hawaiian Holdings Inc.	HA
Haynes Intl. Inc.	HAYN
HB Fuller Co.	FUL
HCA Inc.	HCA
HCC Insurance Hldg. Inc.	HCC
HDFC Bank Ltd.	HDB
Health Care Prop.	HCP
Health Care REIT Inc.	HCN
Health Care Select Sector SPDR	XLV
Health Mgmt. Assoc. Inc. Class A	HMA
Health Net Inc.	HNT
Healthcare Realty Trust Inc.	HR
Healthcare Services Group Inc.	HCSG
HealthSouth Corp.	HLS
HealthSpring Inc.	HS
Healthways Inc.	HWAY
Heartland Payment Systems Inc.	HPY
Heartware International Inc.	HTWR
Heckmann Corp.	HEK
Hecla Mining Co.	HL
HEICO Corp.	HEI

Heidrick & Struggles Inc.	HSII
Heinz Co.	HNZ
Helen of Troy Ltd.	HELE
Helix Energy Solutions	HLX
Helmerich & Payne Inc.	HP
Henry Schein Inc.	HSIC
Herbalife Ltd.	HLF
Hercules Offshore Inc.	HERO
Hercules Technology Growth Capital Inc.	HTGC
Hersha Hospitality REIT Trust	HT
Hershey Foods Corp.	HSY
Hertz Global Holdings Inc.	HTZ
Hess Corp.	HES
Hewlett Packard	HPQ
Hexcel Corp.	HXL
hhgregg Inc.	HGG
Hi Tech Pharmacal Co. Inc.	HITK
Hibbett Sporting Goods Inc.	HIBB
Higher One Inc.	ONE
Highwoods Properties Inc.	HIW
Hillenbrand Inc.	HI
Hill-Rom Holdings Inc.	HRC
Hilltop Holdings Inc.	HTH
Hitachi Ltd. ADR	HIT
Hittite Microwave Corp.	HITT
HMS Holdings Corp.	HMSY
HNI Corp.	HNI
Holly Corp.	HOC
Holly Energy Partners L.P.	HEP
Hollysys Automation Technologies Ltd	HOLI

Hologic Inc.	HOLX
Home Depot Inc.	HD
Home Inns & Hotels Management Inc.	HMIN
Home Properties Inc.	HME
Homebuilders SPDR	XHB
Homex Development Corp.	HXM
Honda Motor Co. Ltd. ADR	HMC
Honeywell Inc.	HON
Horace Mann Educators Corp.	HMN
Hormel Foods Corp.	HRL
Hornbeck Offshore Services Inc.	HOS
Horsehead Holding Corp.	ZINC
Hospira Inc.	HSP
Hospitality Properties Trust	HPT
Host Hotels & Resorts Inc.	HST
Hot Topic Inc.	HOTT
Houston American Energy Corp.	HUSA
Houston Wire & Cable Company	HWCC
Howard Hughes Corp. (The)	HHC
HSBC Hldgs. PLC ADS	HBC
HSN Inc.	HSNI
Huaneng Power Intl. Inc.	HNP
Hub Group Inc.	HUBG
Hubbell Inc. Class B	HUB.B
Hudson City BCP	HCBK
Hudson Pacific Properties Inc.	HPP
Hugoton Royalty Trust	HGT
Human Genome Sciences Inc.	HGSI
Humana Inc.	HUM
Hunt (J.B.) Transport Services Inc.	JBHT

Huntington Bancshares Inc.	HBAN
Huntington Ingalls Industries Inc.	HII
Huntsman Corp.	HUN
Huron Consulting Group Inc.	HURN
Hyatt Hotels Corp.	H
Hypercom Corp.	HYC
Iamgold Corp.	IAG
IberiaBank Corp.	IBKC
ICF International Inc.	ICFI
ICICI Bank Ltd.	IBN
ICON plc	ICLR
Iconix Brand Group Inc.	ICON
ICU Medical	ICUI
Idaho Power Co.	IDA
Idex Corp.	IEX
IDEXX Labs. Inc.	IDXX
IDT Corp.	IDT
IESI-BFC Ltd.	BIN
iGATE Corp.	IGTE
IHS Inc.	IHS
II VI Inc.	IIVI
IIlumina Inc.	ILMN
Illinois Tool Works Inc.	ITW
Imation Corp.	IMN
IMAX Corp.	IMAX
Imergent Inc.	IIG
Immersion Corp.	IMMR
Immucor Inc.	BLUD
ImmunoGen Inc.	IMGN
Impax Laboratories Inc.	IPXL

Imperial Holdings Inc.	IFT
Imperial Oil Ltd.	IMO
Imperial Sugar Co.	IPSU
Incyte Pharma. Inc.	INCY
Independent Bank Corp.	INDB
India Fund Inc.	IFN
Industrial Select Sector SPDR	XLI
Inergy L.P.	NRGY
Infineon Tech ADS	IFNNY
Infinera Corp.	INFN
Infinity Pharmaceuticals Inc.	INFI
Infinity Property and Casualty Corp.	IPCC
Informatica Corp.	INFA
Infospace Inc.	INSP
Infosys Techs. Inc.	INFY
ING Group NV ADS	ING
Ingersoll-Rand Co.	IR
Ingram Micro Inc.	IM
Inland Real Estate Corp.	IRC
InnerWorkings Inc.	INWK
Innophos Holdings Inc	IPHS
Innospec Inc.	IOSP
Innovative Solutions & Support Inc.	ISSC
Inphi Corp.	IPHI
Input/Output Inc.	IO
Insight Enterprises Inc.	NSIT
Insituform Technology Inc.	INSU
Insperity Inc.	NSP
Insteel Industries Inc.	IIIN
Insulet Corp.	PODD

Integra LifeSciences Hlds	IART
Integral Systems Inc.	ISYS
Integrated Device Tech. Inc.	IDTI
Integrated Silicon Solution Inc.	ISSI
Integrys Energy Group Inc.	TEG
Intel Corp.	INTC
Interactive Brokers Group Inc.	IBKR
Interactive Corp.	IACI
Interactive Intelligence Inc.	ININ
interCLICK Inc.	ICLK
Intercontinental Exchange Inc.	ICE
Intercontinental Hotels Group plc	IHG
Interdigital Comms. Corp.	IDCC
Interface Inc.	IFSIA
Interline Brands Inc.	IBI
Intermec Inc.	IN
InterMune Inc.	ITMN
Internap Network Services Corp.	INAP
International Assets Holding Corp.	INTL
International Bancshares Corp.	IBOC
International Paper Co.	IP
International Rectifier Corp.	IRF
International Tower Hill Mines Ltd.	THM
Internet Capital Group Inc.	ICGE
Internet HOLDRs Trust	HHH
Internet Initiative Japan Inc.	IIJI
InterOil Corp.	IOC
Interpublic Grp. of Companies Inc.	IPG
Intersil Hldg. Corp.	ISIL
Interval Leisure Group Inc.	IILG

InterXion Holding NV	INXN
Intevac Inc.	IVAC
Intl. Business Machines	IBM
Intl. Coal Group Inc.	ICO
Intl. Game Tech. Inc.	IGT
Intl. Speedway Corp.	ISCA
Intnl. Flavors & Fragrances Inc.	IFF
IntraLinks Holdings Inc.	IL
Intrepid Potash Inc.	IPI
Intuit Corp.	INTU
Intuitive Surgical Inc.	ISRG
Invacare Corp.	IVC
Invesco Mortgage Capital Inc.	IVR
INVESCO plc	IVZ
Investment Tech. Group Inc. (New)	ITG
Investors Bancorp Inc.	ISBC
Investors Real Estate Trust	IRET
iPath DJ-UBS Agriculture Total Ret. Sub ETN	JJA
iPath DJ-UBS Commodity ETN	DJP
iPath DJ-UBS Copper Tot. Ret. Sub- ETN	JJC
iPath DJ-UBS Grains TR Sub-Idx ETN	JJG
iPath DJ-UBS Livestock Tot. Ret. Sub- ETN	COW
iPath DJ-UBS Natural Gas TR Sub-Idx ETN	GAZ
iPath DJ-UBS Softs Total Return Sub- ETN	JJS
iPath DowJones-UBS Sugar Total Retrun Sub-Indx ETN	SGG
iPath MSCI India ETN	INP
iPath S&P 500 VIX Mid-Term Futures ETN	VXZ
iPath S&P 500 VIX Short-Term Futures ETN	VXX
iPath S&P GSCI Crude Oil TR ETN	OIL
IPG Photonics Corp.	IPGP

IQ Global Agribusiness Small Cap	CROP
Iridium Communications Inc.	IRDM
IRIS Intl. Inc.	IRIS
iRobot Corp.	IRBT
Iron Mountain Inc.	IRM
Ironwood Pharmaceuticals Inc.	IRWD
iShares Barclay 3-7 Year Trsy. Bond	IEI
iShares Barclays 1-3 Year Credit Bond	CSJ
iShares Barclays 7-10 Yr Treasury	IEF
iShares Barclays MBS Bond	MBB
iShares Barclays TIPS Bond	TIP
iShares C&S Realty Majors	ICF
iShares COMEX Gold Trust	IAU
iShares DJ Select Dividend	DVY
iShares DJ Transportation Avg	IYT
iShares DJ U.S. Energy	IYE
iShares DJ U.S. Healthcare	IYH
iShares DJ US Broker-Dealers	IAI
iShares DJ US Financial Sector	IYF
iShares DJ US Home Construction	ITB
iShares DJ US Oil & Gas Exp. & Prod.	IEO
iShares DJ US Real Estate	IYR
iShares DJ US Telecom Sector	IYZ
iShares DJ US Total Market	IYY
iShares DJ US Utilities	IDU
iShares Dow Jones US Basic Materials	IYM
iShares Dow Jones US Financial Services	IYG
iShares Dow Jones US Healthcare Provider	IHF
iShares Dow Jones US Medical Devices	IHI
iShares Dow Jones US Oil Equipment	IEZ

iShares Dow Jones US Regional Banks	IAT
iShares Dow Jones US Tech.	IYW
iShares FTSE/Xinhua China 25	FXI
iShares GS InvesTop Corp. Bond	LQD
iShares GS Networking	IGN
iShares GSCI Commodity-ed	GSG
iShares iBoxx $ High Yield Corp. Bond Fund	HYG
iShares KLD 400 Social	DSI
iShares KLD Select Social	KLD
iShares Lehman 1-3 Yr Treasury	SHY
iShares Lehman 20+ Yr Treasury	TLT
iShares Lehman Aggregate Bond	AGG
iShares MSCI All Country Asia ex Japan	AAXJ
iShares MSCI All Peru Capped	EPU
iShares MSCI Australia	EWA
iShares MSCI Brazil	EWZ
iShares MSCI BRIC	BKF
iShares MSCI Canada	EWC
iShares MSCI Chile Investable Market	ECH
iShares MSCI EAFE	EFA
iShares MSCI EAFE Growth	EFG
iShares MSCI EAFE Small Cap	SCZ
iShares MSCI EAFE Value	EFV
iShares MSCI Emerging Markets	EEM
iShares MSCI Europe Monetary Union	EZU
iShares MSCI Germany	EWG
iShares MSCI Hong Kong	EWH
iShares MSCI Italy	EWI
iShares MSCI Japan	EWJ
iShares MSCI Malaysia	EWM

iShares MSCI Mexico	EWW
iShares MSCI Pacific ex-Japan	EPP
iShares MSCI Singapore	EWS
iShares MSCI South Africa	EZA
iShares MSCI South Korea	EWY
iShares MSCI Spain	EWP
iShares MSCI Sweden	EWD
iShares MSCI Taiwan	EWT
iShares MSCI UK	EWU
iShares Nasdaq Biotechnology	IBB
iShares PHLX Semiconductor	SOXX
iShares Russell 1000	IWB
iShares Russell 1000 Growth	IWF
iShares Russell 1000 Value	IWD
iShares Russell 2000	IWM
iShares Russell 2000 Growth	IWO
iShares Russell 2000 Value	IWN
iShares Russell 3000	IWV
iShares Russell Microcap	IWC
iShares Russell Midcap	IWR
iShares Russell Midcap Growth	IWP
iShares Russell Midcap Value	IWS
iShares S&P 100	OEF
iShares S&P 500	IVV
iShares S&P 500 Growth	IVW
iShares S&P 500 Value	IVE
iShares S&P Emerging Mkts Infrastructure	EMIF
iShares S&P Europe 350	IEV
iShares S&P Global 100	IOO
iShares S&P Global Energy Sector	IXC

iShares S&P GSSI Natural Resources	IGE
iShares S&P India Nifty 50	INDY
iShares S&P Latin Amer. 40	ILF
iShares S&P MidCap 400	IJH
iShares S&P MidCap 400 Growth	IJK
iShares S&P MidCap 400 Value	IJJ
iShares S&P National AMT-Free Muni. Bond	MUB
iShares S&P SmallCap 600	IJR
iShares S&P SmallCap 600	IJS
iShares S&P SmallCap 600 Growth	IJT
iShares S&P U.S. Preferred Stock	PFF
iShares Silver Trust	SLV
Isis Pharmas. Inc.	ISIS
Isle of Capri Casinos Inc.	ISLE
iSoftStone Holdings Limited	ISS
ISTA Pharmaceuticals Inc.	ISTA
iStar Financial Inc.	SFI
ITAU UNIBANCO ADS	ITUB
ITC Holdings Corp.	ITC
Itron Inc.	ITRI
ITT Educ. Srvs. Inc.	ESI
ITT Industries Inc.	ITT
Ivanhoe Mines Ltd.	IVN
IXIA Inc.	XXIA
IXYS Corp.	IXYS
J.M. Smucker Co.	SJM
J.P. Morgan Chase	JPM
j2 Global Coms. Inc.	JCOM
JA Solar Holdings Co. Ltd.	JASO
Jabil Circuit Inc.	JBL

Jack Henry & Associates Inc.	JKHY
Jack in the Box Inc.	JACK
Jacobs Engineering Group Inc.	JEC
Jaguar Mining Inc.	JAG
JAKKS Pacific	JAKK
James River Coal Co.	JRCC
Janus Capital Group Inc.	JNS
Jarden Corp.	JAH
Jazz Pharmaceuticals Inc.	JAZZ
JDA Software Group Inc.	JDAS
JDS Uniphase	JDSU
Jefferies Group Inc.	JEF
JetBlue Airways Corp.	JBLU
JinkoSolar Holding Co. Ltd.	JKS
Jinpan International Ltd.	JST
John Bean Techs. Corp.	JBT
John Wiley & Sons Inc.	JW.A
Johnson & Johnson	JNJ
Johnson Controls Inc.	JCI
Jones Apparel Group Inc.	JNY
Jones Lang Lasalle Inc.	JLL
Jos. A Bank Clothiers Inc.	JOSB
Journal Communications Inc.	JRN
Joy Global Inc.	JOYG
JPMorgan Alerian MLP ETN	AMJ
Juniper Networks Inc.	JNPR
JWH Holding Company LLC	WAC
K12 Inc.	LRN
Kaiser Aluminum Corp.	KALU
Kaman Corp.	KAMN

Kansas City Southern Indus. Inc.	KSU
KapStone Paper and Packaging Corp.	KS
KAR Auction Services Inc.	KAR
Katy Industries Inc.	KT
Kaufman and Broad Home Corp.	KBH
Kaydon Corp.	KDN
KBR Inc.	KBR
KBW Inc.	KBW
KBW Regional Banking	KRE
Keegan Resources Inc.	KGN
Kellogg Co.	K
Kelly Services Inc.	KELYA
KEMET Corp.	KEM
Kendle Intl. Inc.	KNDL
Kenexa Corp.	KNXA
Kennametal Inc.	KMT
Kenneth Cole Prods. Inc.	KCP
Kensey Nash Corp.	KNSY
Key Energy Services Inc.	KEG
KeyCorp	KEY
Keynote Systems Inc.	KEYN
KEYW Holding Corp.	KEYW
Kforce Inc.	KFRC
Kilroy Realty Corp.	KRC
Kimberly-Clark Corp.	KMB
Kimco Realty Corp.	KIM
Kinder Morgan Energy Partners LP	KMP
Kinder Morgan Inc.	KMI
Kinder Morgan Management LLC	KMR
Kindred Healthcare Inc.	KND

Kinetic Concepts Inc.	KCI
Kinross Gold Corp.	KGC
Kirby Corp.	KEX
Kirkland`s Inc.	KIRK
KIT Digital Inc.	KITD
KKR Financial Corp.	KFN
KLA Tencor Corp.	KLAC
Knight Capital Group Inc.	KCG
Knight Transportation Inc.	KNX
Knightsbridge Tankers Ltd.	VLCCF
Knoll Inc.	KNL
Knology Inc.	KNOL
Knot Inc. (The)	KNOT
Kodiak Oil & Gas Corp.	KOG
Kohlberg Capital Corp.	KCAP
Kohlberg Kravis Roberts & Co.	KKR
Kohls Corp.	KSS
KongZhong Corp.	KONG
Koninklijke Philips Electronics NV	PHG
Kookmin Bank	KB
Koppers Holdings Inc.	KOP
Korea Electric Power Corp.	KEP
Korn/Ferry Intl. Inc.	KFY
Kraft Foods Inc.	KFT
Kraton Performance Polymers Inc.	KRA
Kratos Defense & Security Solutions Inc.	KTOS
Krispy Kreme Doughnuts Inc.	KKD
Kroger Co.	KR
K-SEA Transportation Partners LP	KSP
K-Swiss Inc.	KSWS

Kulicke and Soffa Indus. Inc.	KLIC
L & L Energy Inc.	LLEN
L-1 Identity Solutions Inc.	ID
L-3 Communications Inc.	LLL
Lab. Corp. of America Hldgs.	LH
Laclede Group Inc.	LG
Ladish Co. Inc.	LDSH
Lam Research Corp.	LRCX
Lamar Advertising Co.	LAMR
LAN Airlines S.A.	LFL
Lancaster Colony Corp.	LANC
Lance Inc.	LNCE
Landstar System	LSTR
Lannett Co. Inc.	LCI
Las Vegas Sands Corp.	LVS
LaSalle Hotel Properties	LHO
Lattice Semiconductor Corp.	LSCC
Lawson Software Inc.	LWSN
Layne Christensen Co.	LAYN
Lazard Ltd.	LAZ
La-Z-Boy Inc.	LZB
LB Foster Co.	FSTR
LCA Vision Inc.	LCAV
LDK Solar Co. Ltd. ADR	LDK
Le Gaga Holdings Limited	GAGA
Leap Wireless Intl. Inc.	LEAP
Lear Corp.	LEA
LeCroy Corp.	LCRY
Legacy Reserves LP	LGCY
Legg Mason Inc.	LM

Leggett & Platt Inc.	LEG
Lender Processing Services Inc.	LPS
Lennar Corp.	LEN
Lennox Intl.	LII
Leucadia National Corp.	LUK
Lexington Realty Trust	LXP
Lexmark Intl. Grp. Inc. Class A	LXK
LG.Philips LCD Co. Ltd.	LPL
LHC Group Inc.	LHCG
Libbey Inc.	LBY
Liberty Entertainment Group	LSTZA
Liberty Global Inc. Class C	LBTYK
Liberty Media Capital	LCAPA
Liberty Media Interactive	LINTA
Liberty Media Intl. Inc.	LBTYA
Liberty Property Trust	LRY
Life Partners Holdings Inc.	LPHI
Life Technologies Corp.	LIFE
Life Time Fitness Inc.	LTM
LifePoint Hospitals Inc.	LPNT
Ligand Pharma. Inc. Class B	LGND
Lightbridge Corp.	LTBR
Lihua International Inc.	LIWA
Lilly (Eli) and Co.	LLY
Limelight Networks Inc.	LLNW
Limited Inc.	LTD
Lincare Hldgs. Inc.	LNCR
Lincoln Educational Services Corp.	LINC
Lincoln Electric Holdings Inc.	LECO
Lincoln National Corp.	LNC

Lindsay Corp.	LNN
Linear Technology Corp.	LLTC
Linn Energy LLC	LINE
Lions Gate Entertainment Corp.	LGF
Liquidity Services Inc.	LQDT
Lithia Motors Inc.	LAD
Littelfuse Inc.	LFUS
Live Nation Inc.	LYV
LivePerson Inc.	LPSN
Liz Claiborne Inc.	LIZ
LKQ Corp.	LKQX
LM Ericsson Co.	ERIC
Lockheed Martin Corp.	LMT
Loews Corp.	L
Logitech Intl. SA	LOGI
LogMeIn Inc.	LOGM
Longtop Financial Techs. Ltd.	LFT
LoopNet Inc.	LOOP
Loral Space & Comms. Inc.	LORL
Lorillard Inc.	LO
Louisiana-Pacific Corp.	LPX
Lowes Companies Inc.	LOW
LPL Investment Holdings Inc.	LPLA
LSB Industries Inc.	LXU
LSI Industries Inc.	LYTS
LSI Logic Corp.	LSI
LTC Properties Inc.	LTC
LTX-Credence Corp.	LTXC
Lubrizol Corp.	LZ
Lufkin Industries Inc.	LUFK

Lululemon Athletica Inc.	LULU
Lumber Liquidators Inc.	LL
Luminex Corp.	LMNX
Lundin Mining Corp.	LUNMF
Luxottica Group SPA	LUX
LyondellBasell Industries AF S.C.A.	LYB
M&F Worldwide Corp.	MFW
M&T Bank Corp.	MTB
M.D.C. Hldgs. Inc.	MDC
M/I Homes Inc.	MHO
Macerich Co.	MAC
Macquarie Infrastructure Co Trust	MIC
Macys Inc.	M
Madison Square Garden Inc.	MSG
Mag Silver Corp.	MVG
Magellan Health Services Inc.	MGLN
Magellan Midstream Partners L.P.	MMP
Magic Software Enterprises Ltd.	MGIC
Magma Design Automation Inc.	LAVA
Magna Intl. Inc.	MGA
Magnum Hunter Resources Corp.	MHR
Maiden Holdings Ltd.	MHLD
Maidenform Brands Inc.	MFB
MakeMyTrip Limited	MMYT
MAKO Surgical Corp.	MAKO
Manhattan Assoc. Inc.	MANH
Manitowoc Co. Inc.	MTW
Manpower Inc.	MAN
ManTech Intl.	MANT
Manulife Financial Corp.	MFC

MAP Pharmaceuticals Inc.	MAPP
Marchex Inc.	MCHX
Marcus Corp.	MCS
MarineMax Inc.	HZO
Market Vector Brazil Small Cap	BRF
Market Vectors - Gold Miners	GDX
Market Vectors - Steel	SLX
Market Vectors Coal	KOL
Market Vectors India Small-Cap	SCIF
Market Vectors Junior Gold Miners	GDXJ
Market Vectors Nuclear Energy	NLR
Market Vectors RVE Hard Assets Producers	HAP
Market Vectors Solar Energy	KWT
Market Vectors-Agribusiness	MOO
MarketVectors Global Alt. Energy	GEX
MarkWest Energy Partners LP	MWE
Marriott Intl. Inc.	MAR
Marsh & McLennan Companies Inc.	MMC
Marshall & Ilsey Corp.	MI
Marten Transport Ltd.	MRTN
Martin Marietta Materials Inc.	MLM
Marvell Tech. Group Ltd.	MRVL
Masco Corp.	MAS
Masimo Corp.	MASI
Massey Energy Co.	MEE
Mastec Inc.	MTZ
MasterCard Inc.	MA
Materials Select Sector SPDR	XLB
Materion Corp.	MTRN
Matrix Service Co.	MTRX

Mattel Inc.	MAT
Matthews Intl. Corp.	MATW
Maxim Integrated Products Inc.	MXIM
MAXIMUS Inc.	MMS
MaxLinear Inc.	MXL
Maxwell Techs. Inc.	MXWL
Maxygen Inc.	MAXY
MB Financial Inc.	MBFI
MBIA Inc.	MBI
McCormick & Schmicks Seafood Rest. Inc.	MSSR
McCormick Co	MKC
McDermott Intl. Inc.	MDR
McDonalds Corp.	MCD
MCG Capital Corp.	MCGC
McGraw-Hill Co. Inc.	MHP
McKesson Corp.	MCK
McMoran Exploration Co.	MMR
MDU Resources Group Inc.	MDU
Mead Johnson Nutrition Co.	MJN
Meadowbrook Insurance Group Inc.	MIG
MeadWestvaco Corp.	MWV
Measurement Specialties Inc.	MEAS
Mechel Open Joint Stock Co.	MTL
Mecox Lane Ltd.	MCOX
Medallion Financial Corp	TAXI
MedAssets Inc.	MDAS
MedCath Corp.	MDTH
Medco Health Solutions Inc.	MHS
Medical Properties Trust Inc.	MPW
Medicis Pharmaceutical Corp.	MRX

Medidata Solutions Inc.	MDSO
Medifast Inc.	MED
Medivation Inc.	MDVN
MEDNAX Inc.	MD
MedQuist Inc.	MEDQ
Medtronic Inc.	MDT
Melco PBL Entertainment (Macau) Ltd.	MPEL
Mellanox Techs. Ltd.	MLNX
MEMC Electronic Materials Inc.	WFR
Mens Wearhouse	MW
Mentor Graphics Corp.	MENT
Mercadolibre Inc.	MELI
Mercer International Inc.	MERC
Merck & Co. Inc.	MRK
Mercury Computer Systems Inc.	MRCY
Mercury General Corp.	MCY
Meredith Corp.	MDP
Merge Techs. Inc.	MRGE
Meridian Bioscience Inc.	VIVO
Merit Medical Systems Inc.	MMSI
Meritage Corp.	MTH
Meritor Inc.	MTOR
Meru Networks Inc.	MERU
Mesabi Trust	MSB
Metabolix Inc.	MBLX
Metalico Inc.	MEA
Metals USA Holdings Corp.	MUSA
Methanex Corp.	MEOH
Methode Electronics Inc.	MEI
MetLife Inc.	MET

MetroPCS Comms. Inc.	PCS
Mettler-Toledo Intl. Inc.	MTD
MF Global Ltd.	MF
MFA Mortgage Investments Inc.	MFA
MGIC Investments Corp.	MTG
MGM Mirage	MGM
MGP Ingredients Inc.	MGPI
Micrel Inc.	MCRL
Microchip Technology Inc.	MCHP
Micromet Inc.	MITI
Micron Technology Inc.	MU
Micros Systems Inc.	MCRS
Microsemi Corp.	MSCC
Microsoft Corp.	MSFT
Microstrategy Inc.	MSTR
Mid-America Apartment Communities Inc.	MAA
Midas Inc.	MDS
Middleby Corp.	MIDD
Miller (Herman) Inc.	MLHR
Miller Petroleum Inc.	MILL
Millicom Intnl. Cellular SA	MICC
MIM Corp.	BIOS
Mindray Medical Intl. Ltd.	MR
Mindspeed Technologies Inc.	MSPD
Mine Safety Appliances Co.	MSA
Minefinders Corp. Ltd.	MFN
Minerals Techs. Inc.	MTX
MIPS Technologies Inc.	MIPS
Mitel Networks Corp.	MITL
Mittal Steel Co. N.V.	MT

MKS Instruments Inc.	MKSI
Mobile Mini Inc.	MINI
Mobile Telesys. OJSC ADR	MBT
Modine Manufacturing Co.	MOD
Moduslink Global Solutions Inc.	MLNK
Mohawk Indus.	MHK
Molex Inc.	MOLX
Molina Healthcare Inc.	MOH
Molson Coors Brewing Co.	TAP
Molycorp Inc.	MCP
Momenta Pharmas. Inc.	MNTA
Monarch Casino & Resort Inc.	MCRI
Monolithic Power Systems Inc.	MPWR
Monotype Imaging Holdings Inc.	TYPE
Monro Muffler Brake Inc.	MNRO
Monsanto Co.	MON
Monster Worldwide Inc.	MWW
Montpelier Re Holdings Ltd.	MRH
Moodys Corp.	MCO
Moog Inc.	MOG.A
Morgan Stanley	MS
Morgan Stanley India Investment Fund Inc.	IIF
Morgans Hotel Group Co.	MHGC
Morningstar Inc.	MORN
Mosaic Co.	MOS
Motorola Mobility Inc.	MMI
Motorola Solutions Inc.	MSI
Motricity Inc.	MOTR
Movado Group Inc.	MOV
MSC Industrial Direct Co. Inc.	MSM

MSCI Inc.	MSCI
Mueller Industries Inc.	MLI
Multi-Fineline Electronix Inc.	MFLX
Multimedia Games Inc.	MGAM
Murphy Oil Corp.	MUR
MVC Capital Inc.	MVC
MWI Veterinary Supply Inc.	MWIV
Myers Industries Inc.	MYE
Mylan Labs.	MYL
MYR Group Inc.	MYRG
Myriad Genetics Inc.	MYGN
Nabi BioPharm.	NABI
Nabors Indus. Inc.	NBR
Nalco Holding Co.	NLC
Nam Tai Electronics Inc.	NTE
Nanometrics Inc.	NANO
Nara Bancorp Inc.	NARA
Nasdaq Stock Market Inc.	NDAQ
Nash Finch Co.	NAFC
National Beverage Corp.	FIZZ
National CineMedia Inc.	NCMI
National Financial Partners Corp.	NFP
National Fuel Gas Co.	NFG
National Instruments Corp.	NATI
National Oilwell Varco Inc.	NOV
National Penn Bancshares Inc.	NPBC
National Retail Properties Inc.	NNN
National Semiconductor Corp.	NSM
Nationwide Health Properties Inc.	NHP
Natural Gas Srvs. Group Inc.	NGS

Natural Resource Partners LP	NRP
Natus Medical Inc.	BABY
Navigant Consulting Inc.	NCI
Navigators Group Inc.	NAVG
Navios Maritime Holdings Inc.	NM
Navios Maritime Partners LP	NMM
Navistar Intl. Corp.	NAV
NBT Bancorp Inc.	NBTB
NCI Building Systems Inc.	NCS
NCR Corp.	NCR
Neenah Paper Inc.	NP
Nektar Therapeutics	NKTR
Nelnet Inc.	NNI
NeoPhotonics Corp.	NPTN
Ness Techs. Inc.	NSTC
Net 1 U.E.P.S. Techs. Inc.	UEPS
Net Servios de Comunicao SA	NETC
Netease.com Inc. ADR	NTES
NETGEAR Inc.	NTGR
NetLogic Microsystems Inc.	NETL
NetScout Systems Inc.	NTCT
NetSpend Holdings Inc.	NTSP
NetSuite Inc.	N
Network Appliance Corp.	NTAP
Neurocrine Bios	NBIX
NeuStar Inc.	NSR
Neutral Tandem Inc.	TNDM
Nevsun Resources Ltd.	NSU
New Gold Inc.	NGD
New Jersey Resources Corp.	NJR

New Oriental Educ. & Tech. Group Inc.	EDU
New York & Company Inc.	NWY
New York Community Bancorp Inc.	NYB
New York Times Co. Class A	NYT
Newcastle Investment Corp.	NCT
Newell Rubbermaid Inc.	NWL
Newfield Exploration Co.	NFX
NewMarket Corp.	NEU
Newmont Mining Corp.	NEM
Newpark Resources Inc.	NR
Newport Corp.	NEWP
News Corp. Ltd. (The) Class A	NWSA
News Corp. Ltd. (The) Class B	NWS
Nexen Inc.	NXY
NextEra Energy Inc.	NEE
Nextgen Group plc	NGG
NGP Capital Resources Co.	NGPC
NIC Inc.	EGOV
NICE Systems Ltd.	NICE
NICOR Inc.	GAS
Nielsen Holdings N.V.	NLSN
NII Hldgs. Inc.	NIHD
Nike Inc.	NKE
Nippon Telegraph and Telephone Corp.	NTT
Niska Gas Storage Partners LLC	NKA
NiSource Inc.	NI
Nissan Motors AD	NSANY
Nlix Inc.	NFLX
NN Inc.	NNBR
Noah Holdings Ltd. ADR	NOAH

Noble Affiliates Inc.	NBL
Noble Drilling Corp.	NE
Nokia Corp. ADR	NOK
Nomura Holdings Inc.	NMR
Noranda Aluminum Holding Corp.	NOR
Nordic American Tanker Shipping Ltd.	NAT
Nordion Inc.	NDZ
Nordson Corp.	NDSN
Nordstrom Inc.	JWN
Norfolk Southern Corp.	NSC
North American Energy Partners Inc.	NOA
North American Palladium	PAL
Northeast Utils.	NU
Northern Dynasty Minerals Ltd.	NAK
Northern Oil and Gas Inc.	NOG
Northern Trust Corp.	NTRS
Northrop Grumman Corp.	NOC
NorthStar Realty Finance Corp.	NRF
Northwest Bancorp Inc.	NWBI
Northwest Natural Gas Co.	NWN
Northwest Pipe Co.	NWPX
Northwestern Corp.	NWE
Nova Measuring Instruments Ltd.	NVMI
Novagold Resources Inc.	NG
Novartis AG	NVS
Novatel Wireless Inc.	NVTL
Novellus Systems Inc.	NVLS
Novo Nordisk A/S	NVO
NPS Pharma. Inc.	NPSP
NRG Energy Inc.	NRG

NSTAR	NST
NTT DoCoMo Inc.	DCM
Nu Skin Enterprises Inc.	NUS
Nuance Comms.	NUAN
Nucor Corp.	NUE
NuStar Energy LP	NS
NuStar GP Holdings LLC	NSH
NutriSystem Inc.	NTRI
NuVasive Inc.	NUVA
NV Energy Inc.	NVE
NVIDIA Corp.	NVDA
NXP Semiconductors N.V.	NXPI
Nxstage Medical Inc.	NXTM
NYSE Group Inc.	NYX
O`Charley`s Inc.	CHUX
O2Micro Intl. Ltd.	OIIM
Oasis Petroleum Inc.	OAS
Obagi Medical Products Inc.	OMPI
Occidental Petroleum Corp.	OXY
Oceaneering Intl. Inc.	OII
Oclaro Inc.	OCLR
Ocwen Financial Corp.	OCN
Ocz Technology Group Inc.	OCZ
Officemax Inc.	OMX
OGE Energy Corp.	OGE
Oil Services HOLDRs Trust	OIH
Oil States Intl. Inc.	OIS
Old Dominion Freight Line Inc.	ODFL
Old National Bancorp	ONB
Old Republic International Corp.	ORI

Olin Corp.	OLN
Olympic Steel Inc.	ZEUS
OM Group Inc.	OMG
Omega Healthcare Investors Inc. REIT	OHI
Omega Protein Corp.	OME
Omnicare Inc.	OCR
Omnicell Inc. CA	OMCL
Omnicom Group Inc.	OMC
OmniVision Tech. Inc.	OVTI
OMNOVA Solutions Inc.	OMN
On Assignment Inc.	ASGN
On Semiconductor Corp.	ONNN
OncoGenex Pharmaceuticals Inc.	OGXI
Oncolytics Biotech Inc.	ONCY
OneBeacon Insurance Group Ltd.	OB
ONEOK Inc.	OKE
ONEOK Partners L.P.	OKS
Onyx Pharma.	ONXX
Open Text Corp.	OTEX
OpenTable Inc.	OPEN
Oplink Comms. Inc.	OPLK
OPNET Technologies Inc.	OPNT
Optimer Pharma. Inc.	OPTR
optionsXpress Holdings Inc.	OXPS
Oracle Corp.	ORCL
OraSure Tech.	OSUR
Orbital Sciences Corp.	ORB
Orbotech Ltd.	ORBK
OReilly Automotive Inc	ORLY
Oriental Financial Group Inc.	OFG

Orient-Express Hotels Ltd.	OEH
Origin Agritech Ltd.	SEED
Orion Marine Group Inc	ORN
Oritani Financial Corp.	ORIT
Ormat Techs. Inc.	ORA
Oshkosh Truck Corp.	OSK
OSI Systems Inc.	OSIS
Osiris Therapeutics Inc.	OSIR
Otter Tail Corp.	OTTR
Overseas Shipholding Group	OSG
Overstock.com Inc.	OSTK
Owens & Minor Inc.	OMI
Owens Corning Sales Inc.	OC
Owens-Illinois Inc.	OI
Oxford Indus. Inc.	OXM
OZ Management LLC	OZM
P.F. Changs China Bistro	PFCB
PAA Natural Gas Storage LP	PNG
PACCAR Inc.	PCAR
Pacer Intl. Inc.	PACR
Pacific Biosciences of California Inc.	PACB
Pacific Capital Bancorp	PCBC
Packaging Corp. of America	PKG
PacWest Bancorp	PACW
Pain Therapeutics Inc.	PTIE
Pall Corp.	PLL
Palomar Medical Techs. Inc.	PMTI
Pan American Silver Inc.	PAAS
Panasonic Corp.	PC
Panera Bread Co.	PNRA

Pantry Inc. (The)	PTRY
Papa Johns International Inc.	PZZA
Parametric Tech. Corp.	PMTC
PAREXEL International Corp	PRXL
Park Electrochemical Corp.	PKE
Parker Drilling Co.	PKD
Parker-Hannifin Corp.	PH
Parkway Properties Inc.	PKY
PartnerRe Ltd.	PRE
Patni Computer Systems Ltd.	PTI
Patriot Coal Corp.	PCX
Patterson Dental Co.	PDCO
Patterson Energy Inc	PTEN
Paychex Inc.	PAYX
Payless ShoeSource Inc.	PSS
PDL BioPharma Inc.	PDLI
Peabody Energy Corp.	BTU
Pearson plc	PSO
Peets Coffee & Tea Inc.	PEET
Pegasystems Inc.	PEGA
Pengrowth Energy Trust	PGH
Penn National Gaming Inc	PENN
Penn Virginia Corp.	PVA
Penn Virginia Resource Partners LP	PVR
Penn West Energy Trust	PWE
Pennantpark Investment Corp.	PNNT
Penney (J.C.) Co. Inc.	JCP
Pennsylvania REIT	PEI
PennyMac Mortgage Investment Trust	PMT
Penske Automotive Group Inc.	PAG

Penson Worldwide Inc.	PNSN
Pentair Inc.	PNR
Peoples United Fin. Inc.	PBCT
Pep Boys-Manny Moe & Jack Inc.	PBY
PepsiCo Inc.	PEP
Perfect World Co. Ltd.	PWRD
Perficient Inc.	PRFT
Pericom Semiconductor Corp.	PSEM
Perkin Elmer Instr.	PKI
Permian Basin Royalty Trust	PBT
Perrigo Co.	PRGO
Perry Ellis International Inc.	PERY
PetMed Express Inc.	PETS
Petrobras Energia Participaciones SA	PZE
PetroChina Co. Ltd.	PTR
Petrohawk Energy Corp.	HK
Petroleo Brasileiro SA	PBR
Petroleo Brasileiro SA	PBR.A
Petroleum Development Corp.	PETD
PetroQuest Energy Inc.	PQ
PetsMart Inc.	PETM
Pfizer Inc.	PFE
PFSweb Inc.	PFSW
PG&E Corp.	PCG
PH Glatfelter Co.	GLT
Pharma. Prod. Dev.	PPDI
Pharmaceutical HOLDRs Trust	PPH
Pharmaceutical Resources Inc.	PRX
Pharmacopeia Inc.	ACCL
Pharmacyclics Inc.	PCYC

Pharmasset Inc.	VRUS
Pharmerica Corp.	PMC
PHH Corp.	PHH
Philip Morris Intl. Inc.	PM
Philippine Long Distance Telephone Co.	PHI
Phillips-Van Heusen Corp.	PVH
Photronics Inc.	PLAB
PICO Holdings Inc.	PICO
Piedmont Natural Gas Co. Inc.	PNY
Piedmont Office Realty Trust Inc.	PDM
Pier 1 Imports Inc.	PIR
Pike Electric Corp.	PIKE
Pilgrim`s Pride Corp.	PPC
PIMCO 1-3 Year U.S. Treasury Fund	TUZ
Pinnacle Airlines Corp.	PNCL
Pinnacle Entertainment Inc.	PNK
Pinnacle Financial Partners Inc.	PNFP
Pinnacle West Capital Corp.	PNW
Pioneer Drilling Co.	PDC
Pioneer Natural Resources Co.	PXD
Piper Jaffray Co.	PJC
Pitney Bowes Inc.	PBI
Plains All American Pipeline LP	PAA
Plains Exploration & Prod. Co. L.P.	PXP
Plantronics Inc	PLT
Platinum Underwriters Hldgs. Ltd.	PTP
Plexus Corp.	PLXS
Plum Creek Timber Co. LP	PCL
PMC-Sierra Inc.	PMCS
PNC Bank Corp.	PNC

PNM Resources Inc.	PNM
Polaris Industries Inc.	PII
Polycom Inc.	PLCM
PolyOne Corp.	POL
Polypore International Inc.	PPO
Portfolio Recovery Assoc. Inc.	PRAA
Portland General Electric	POR
POSCO ADR	PKX
Post Properties Inc.	PPS
Potash Corp. of Saskatchewan Inc.	POT
Potlatch Corp.	PCH
Potomac Electric Power Co.	POM
Powell Industries Inc.	POWL
Power Integrations Inc.	POWI
Power-One Inc.	PWER
PowerSecure Intl. Inc.	POWR
PowerShares CEF Income Composite	PCEF
PowerShares DB Agriculture	DBA
PowerShares DB Base Metals	DBB
PowerShares DB Commodity Tracking	DBC
PowerShares DB Energy	DBE
PowerShares DB G10 Currency Harvest	DBV
PowerShares DB Gold	DGL
PowerShares DB Oil	DBO
PowerShares DB Precious Metals	DBP
PowerShares DB Silver	DBS
PowerShares DB US Dollar Bullish	UUP
PowerShares Dividend Achiever	PFM
PowerShares DWA Technical Leaders	PDP
PowerShares Dynamic Banking	PJB

PowerShares Dynamic Energy Expl. & Prod.	PXE
PowerShares Dynamic Leisure & Entertainment	PEJ
PowerShares Dynamic Lg. Cap. Value	PWV
PowerShares Dynamic Networking Intellidex	PXQ
PowerShares Dynamic Oil Services	PXJ
PowerShares Dynamic Small Cap. Growth	PWT
PowerShares Dynamic Small Cap. Value	PWY
PowerShares Dynamic Technology Sector	PTF
PowerShares Emerging Mkts Sovereign Debt	PCY
PowerShares Financial Preferred	PGF
PowerShares FTSE RAFI US 1000	PRF
PowerShares Fundamental High Yld Corp Bond	PHB
PowerShares Global Water	PIO
PowerShares India Portfolio	PIN
PowerShares Insured National Muni Bond	PZA
PowerShares ML Fixed Rate Pref. Sec.	PGX
Powershares S&P 500 BuyWrite	PBP
PowerShares Short DB US Dollar	UDN
PowerShares Water Resources	PHO
PowerShares WilderHill Clean Energy	PBW
PowerShrs. Gold Dragon USX China	PGJ
POZEN Inc.	POZN
PPG Indus. Inc.	PPG
PPL Corp.	PPL
Praxair Inc.	PX
Precision Castparts Corp.	PCP
Precision Drilling Trust	PDS
Premiere Global Srvs. Inc.	PGI
Pre-Paid Legal Services Inc.	PPD
Prestige Brands Holdings Inc.	PBH

Priceline.com Inc.	PCLN
PriceSmart Inc.	PSMT
Pride Intl. Inc.	PDE
Primerica Inc.	PRI
Principal Financial Group Inc.	PFG
PrivateBancorp Inc.	PVTB
ProAssurance Corp.	PRA
Procera Networks Inc.	PKT
Procter & Gamble Co.	PG
Progenics Pharmaceuticals Inc.	PGNX
Progresive Techs. Inc.	PGR
Progress Energy Inc.	PGN
Progress Software Corp.	PRGS
ProLogis	PLD
ProShares Credit Suisse 130/30	CSM
ProShares Short 20+ Year Treasury Bonde	TBF
ProShares Short DJ US Financials	SEF
ProShares Short Dow 30	DOG
ProShares Short QQQ	PSQ
ProShares Short S&P 500	SH
ProShares ULTRA 20 Plus Year Treasury	UBT
ProShares Ultra Basic Materials	UYM
ProShares Ultra DJ US Semiconductor	USD
ProShares Ultra DJ-AIG Crude Oil	UCO
ProShares Ultra Dow 30	DDM
ProShares Ultra Dow Jones U.S. Indus.	UXI
ProShares Ultra Euro	ULE
ProShares Ultra Financial	UYG
ProShares Ultra FTSE/Xinhua China 25	XPP
ProShares Ultra Gold	UGL

ProShares Ultra MCSI Emerging Mkts.	EET
ProShares Ultra Oil & Gas	DIG
ProShares ULTRA PRO DOW 30	UDOW
ProShares ULTRA PRO MidCap 400	UMDD
ProShares ULTRA PRO Russell 2000	URTY
ProShares Ultra Pro S&P 500	UPRO
ProShares ULTRA PRO SHORT DOW 30	SDOW
ProShares ULTRA PRO SHORT MidCap 400	SMDD
ProShares ULTRA PRO SHORT Russell 2000	SRTY
ProShares Ultra Pro SHORT S&P 500	SPXU
ProShares ULTRA QQQQ	TQQQ
ProShares Ultra Real Estate	URE
ProShares Ultra Russell 2000	UWM
ProShares Ultra S&P 500	SSO
ProShares Ultra S&P MidCap400	MVV
ProShares Ultra Short MCSI Brazil	BZQ
ProShares Ultra Silver	AGQ
ProShares Ultra SmallCap 600	SAA
ProShares UltraShort Basic Materials	SMN
ProShares UltraShort DJ US Industrials	SIJ
ProShares UltraShort DJ-AIG Crude Oil	SCO
ProShares UltraShort Dow 30	DXD
ProShares UltraShort Euro	EUO
ProShares UltraShort Financials	SKF
ProShares UltraShort FTSE Xinhua China 25	FXP
ProShares UltraShort Gold	GLL
ProShares UltraShort Lehman 20+ Treasury	TBT
ProShares UltraShort Lehman 7-10 Yr Trsy	PST
ProShares UltraShort MSCI EAFE	EFU
ProShares UltraShort MSCI Emerging Markets	EEV

ProShares UltraShort MSCI Europe	EPV
ProShares UltraShort MSCI Japan	EWV
ProShares UltraShort Oil & Gas	DUG
ProShares UltraShort QQQQ	SQQQ
ProShares UltraShort Real Estate	SRS
ProShares UltraShort Russell 2000	TWM
ProShares UltraShort S&P 500	SDS
ProShares UltraShort S&P MidCap 400	MZZ
ProShares UltraShort Semiconductor	SSG
ProShares UltraShort Silver	ZSL
ProShares VIX Mid-Term Futures	VIXM
ProShares VIX Short-Term Futures	VIXY
Prospect Capital Corp.	PSEC
Prosperity Bancshares Inc.	PRSP
Protalix BioTherapeutics Inc.	PLX
Protective Life Corp.	PL
Provident Energy Trust	PVX
Provident Financial Services Inc.	PFS
Provident New York Bancorp	PBNY
Prudential Financial Inc.	PRU
Prudential PLC	PUK
PS Business Parks Inc.	PSB
PSS World Med Inc.	PSSI
PT Telekomunikasi Indonesia ADR	TLK
Public Service Enterprise Group Inc.	PEG
Public Storage Inc.	PSA
Pulse Electronics Corp.	PULS
Pulte Corp.	PHM
Quanex Building Products Corp.	NX
Quanta Services Inc.	PWR

Quest Dignostics Inc.	DGX
Questar Corp.	STR
Quicksilver Resources Inc.	KWK
Randgold Resources Ltd.	GOLD
Realty Income Corp.	O
ReneSola Ltd.	SOL
Rockwell Collins Inc.	COL
Rydex Russell Top 50	XLG
S Physical Silver Shares	SIVR
S Physical Swiss Gold Shares	SGOL
S&P Depositary Receipts Trust	SPY
S&P Midcap 400 SPDR	MDY
S&T Bancorp Inc.	STBA
S1 Corp.	SONE
Saba Software Inc.	SABA
Sabra Healthcare REIT Inc.	SBRA
Safeguard Scientifics Inc.	SFE
Safety Insurance Group Inc.	SAFT
Safeway Inc.	SWY
Saia Inc.	SAIA
SAIC Inc.	SAI
Saks Inc.	SKS
salesforce.com Inc.	CRM
Salix Pharma. Inc.	SLXP
Sally Beauty Holdings Inc.	SBH
San Juan Basin Royalty Trust	SJT
Sanderson Farms Inc.	SAFM
SanDisk Corp.	SNDK
SandRidge Energy Inc.	SD
Sangamo Biosciences Inc.	SGMO

Sanmina-SCI Corp.	SANM
Sanofi-Synthelabo	SNY
SAP AG	SAP
Sapient Corp.	SAPE
Sappi Ltd.	SPP
Sara Lee Corp.	SLE
Sasol Ltd.	SSL
Sauer-Danfoss Inc.	SHS
Savient Pharmas. Inc.	SVNT
SAVVIS Inc.	SVVS
SBA Comms. Corp.	SBAC
SCANA Corp.	SCG
ScanSource Inc.	SCSC
Schlumberger Ltd.	SLB
Schnitzer Steel Indus. Inc.	SCHN
Scholastic Corp.	SCHL
School Specialty Inc.	SCHS
Schwab Emerging Markets Equity	SCHE
Schwab Intermediate-Term US Treasury	SCHR
Schwab International Equity	SCHF
Schwab International Small Cap Equity	SCHC
Schwab Short-Term US Treasury	SCHO
Schwab US Broad-Market	SCHB
Schwab US Large Cap. Growth	SCHG
Schwab US Large Cap. Value	SCHV
Schwab US Large-Cap.	SCHX
Schwab US Small-Cap.	SCHA
Schwab US TIPs	SCHP
Schweitzer-Mauduit International Inc.	SWM
Scientific Games Corp.	SGMS

Scotts Co. Class A	SMG
SCP Pool Corp.	POOL
Scripps Networks Interactive Inc.	SNI
Seabridge Gold Inc.	SA
Seachange Intern.	SEAC
Seacor Holdings Inc.	CKH
SeaDrill Limited	SDRL
Seagate Tech.	STX
Seahawk Drilling Inc.	HAWKQ
Sealed Air Corp.	SEE
Sears Holdings Corp.	SHLD
Seaspan Corp.	SSW
Seattle Genetics Inc.	SGEN
SEI Investments Co.	SEIC
Select Comfort Corp.	SCSS
Select Medical Holdings Corp.	SEM
Selective Insurance Group Inc.	SIGI
Semiconductor HOLDRs Trust	SMH
Sempra Energy	SRE
Semtech Corp.	SMTC
Senior Housing Properties Trust	SNH
Senomyx Inc.	SNMX
Sensata Technologies Holding NV	ST
Sensient Techs. Corp.	SXT
Sequenom Inc.	SQNM
Service Corp Intl.	SCI
ServiceSource International LLC	SREV
Shanda Games Limited	GAME
Shanda Interactive Ent. Ltd.	SNDA
Shaw Group Inc.	SHAW

Sherwin-Williams Co.	SHW
Ship Finance Intl. Ltd.	SFL
Shire PLC	SHPGY
ShoreTel Inc.	SHOR
Shuffle Master Inc.	SHFL
Shutterfly Inc.	SFLY
Siemens AG	SI
Sierra Wireless Inc.	SWIR
Sify Technologies Limited	SIFY
SIGA Techs. Inc.	SIGA
Sigma Designs Inc.	SIGM
Sigma-Aldrich Corp.	SIAL
Signature Bank	SBNY
Signet Jewelers Limited	SIG
Silgan Holdings Inc.	SLGN
Silicon Graphics Intl.	SGI
Silicon Image Inc.	SIMG
Silicon Labs	SLAB
Silicon Motion Tech. Corp.	SIMO
Siliconware Precision Indus. Co. Ltd.	SPIL
Silver Standard Res. Inc.	SSRI
Silver Wheaton Corp.	SLW
Silvercorp Metals Inc.	SVM
Simcere Pharmaceutical Group.	SCR
Simon Property Group Inc.	SPG
Simple Tech Inc.	STEC
Simpson Manufacturing Co. Inc.	SSD
Sims Group Ltd.	SMS
Sina Corp.	SINA
Sinclair Broadcast Group	SBGI

SinoCoking Coal and Coke Chemical	SCOK
Sinopec Corp.	SNP
Sinopec Shanghai Petrochemical Co. Ltd.	SHI
SinoTech Energy Ltd. ADR	CTE
Sirona Dental Systems Inc.	SIRO
Six Flags Entertainment Corp.	SIX
Sk Telecom Co. Ltd. ADS	SKM
Skechers USA Inc.	SKX
Skilled Healthcare Group Inc.	SKH
Sky-Mobi Ltd. ADR	MOBI
SkyWest Inc.	SKYW
SkyWorks Solutions Inc.	SWKS
SL Green Realty Corp.	SLG
SLM Hldg. Corp.	SLM
SMART Modular Technologies (WWH) Inc.	SMOD
Smart Technologies Inc.	SMT
Smith & Nephew PLC	SNN
Smith Micro Software Inc.	SMSI
Smithfield Foods	SFD
Smurfit-Stone Container Corp.	SSCC
Snap-On Inc.	SNA
SodaStream International Ltd.	SODA
Software HOLDRs Trust	SWH
Sohu.com Inc.	SOHU
Solar Capital Ltd.	SLRC
Solarfun Power Holdings Co. Ltd.	HSOL
SolarWinds Inc.	SWI
Solera Holdings Inc.	SLH
Solutia Inc.	SOA
Sonic Automotive Inc.	SAH

Sonic Corp.	SONC
Sonoco Products Co.	SON
SonoSite Inc.	SONO
Sony Corp. ADR	SNE
Sothebys Hlds. Inc.	BID
Sourcefire Inc.	FIRE
South Jersey Industries Inc.	SJI
Southern Co.	SO
Southern Copper Corp.	SCCO
Southern Union Co.	SUG
Southwest Airlines Co.	LUV
Southwest Bancorp Inc.	OKSB
Southwest Gas Corp.	SWX
Southwest Securities Group Inc.	SWS
Southwestern Energy Co.	SWN
Sovran Self Storage Inc.	SSS
Spansion Inc.	CODE
Spartan Motors Inc.	SPAR
Spartan Stores Inc.	SPTN
Spartech Corp.	SEH
SPDR Lehman High Yield Bond	JNK
SPDR Lehman Intl Treasury Bond	BWX
SPDR Lehman Municipal Bond	TFI
SPDR S&P China	GXC
SPDR S&P Emerging Europe	GUR
SPDR S&P Hi Yield Dividend Arist.	SDY
SPDR S&P International Dividend	DWX
SPDR S&P Retail	XRT
SPDR S&P Semiconductor Select Industry	XSD
Spectra Energy	SE

Spectra Energy Partners LP	SEP
Spectranetics Corp.	SPNC
Spectrum Pharma. Inc.	SPPI
Spherion Corp.	SFN
Spirit AeroSystems Holdings Inc.	SPR
Spreadtrum Communications Inc.	SPRD
Sprint Nextel Corp.	S
SPX Corp.	SPW
SRA Intl. Inc.	SRX
SS&C Technologies Holdings Inc.	SSNC
St Joe Co. (The)	JOE
St. Jude Medical Inc.	STJ
St. Mary Land & Exploration Co.	SM
Staar Surgical Co.	STAA
Stage Stores Inc.	SSI
Stamps.com Inc.	STMP
StanCorp Financial Group Inc.	SFG
Standard Microsystems Corp.	SMSC
Standard Motor Products Inc.	SMP
Stanley Works	SWK
Staples Inc.	SPLS
Starbucks Corp.	SBUX
StarTek Inc.	SRT
Starwood Hotels & Resorts Worldwide Inc.	HOT
Starwood Property Trust Inc.	STWD
State Street Boston Corp.	STT
Statoil ASA	STO
Steel Dynamics Inc.	STLD
Steelcase Inc-Class A	SCS
Stein Mart Inc.	SMRT

Stericycle Inc.	SRCL
Steris Corp.	STE
Sterling Bancorp	STL
Sterling Bancshares Inc.	SBIB
Sterling Construction Co. Inc.	STRL
Sterling Financial Corp.	STSA
Sterlite Industries India Ltd.	SLT
Steven Madden Ltd.	SHOO
Stewart Enterprises Inc.	STEI
Stewart Information Services Corp.	STC
Stifel Financial Corp.	SF
Stillwater Mining Co.	SWC
STMicroelectronics N.V.	STM
Stone Energy Corp.	SGY
Stonemor Partners LP	STON
Stoneridge Inc.	SRI
STR Holdings Inc.	STRI
Stratasys Inc.	SSYS
Strategic Hotels & Resorts Inc.	BEE
Strayer Education Inc.	STRA
streetTRACKS Gold Shares	GLD
streetTRACKS KBW Bank	KBE
streetTRACKS KBW Capital Markets	KCE
streetTRACKS KBW Insurance	KIE
streetTracks SPDR Metals and Mining	XME
streetTracks SPDR Oil & Gas Equip & Srvcs	XES
streetTracks SPDR Oil & Gas Expl & Drill	XOP
streetTracks SPDR S&P BRIC 40	BIK
Stryker Corp.	SYK
Subsea 7 SA ADR	SUBCY

Suburban Propane Partners LP	SPH
SuccessFactors Inc.	SFSF
Summit Hotel Properties Inc.	INN
Sun Co. Inc.	SUN
Sun Communities Inc.	SUI
Sun Healthcare Group Inc.	SUNH
Sun Life Fin. Srvs. of Canada Inc.	SLF
Sun Trust Banks Inc.	STI
Suncor Energy Inc.	SU
Sunoco Logistics Partners LP	SXL
SunOpta Inc.	STKL
SunPower Corp. Class A	SPWRA
SunPower Corp. Class B	SPWRB
Sunrise Assisted Living Inc	SRZ
Sunstone Hotel Investors Inc.	SHO
Suntech Power Co. Ltd.	STP
Super Micro Computer Inc.	SMCI
Superior Energy Srvs. Inc.	SPN
Superior Indus. Intl. Inc.	SUP
Supertex Inc.	SUPX
Supervalu Inc.	SVU
support.com Inc.	SPRT
Surmodics Inc.	SRDX
Susquehanna Bancshares Inc.	SUSQ
SVB Financial Group	SIVB
Swift Energy Co.	SFY
Swift Transportation Co. Inc.	SWFT
Swisher Hygiene Inc.	SWSH
SXC Health Solutions Corp.	SXCI
Sycamore Networks Inc.	SCMR

Sykes Enterprises Inc.	SYKE
Symantec Corp.	SYMC
Symetra Financial Corp.	SYA
Symmetricom Inc.	SYMM
Symmetry Medical Inc.	SMA
Synaptics Inc.	SYNA
Synchronoss Techs. Inc.	SNCR
Synergetics USA Inc.	SURG
Syneron Medical Ltd.	ELOS
Syngenta AG	SYT
SYNNEX Corp.	SNX
Synopsys Inc.	SNPS
Synovis Life Techs. Inc.	SYNO
Synta Pharmaceuticals Corp.	SNTA
Syntel Inc.	SYNT
Sysco Corp.	SYY
Systemax Inc.	SYX
T. Rowe Price Associates	TROW
Taiwan Semicon. Manuf. Co. Ltd.	TSM
Take-Two Interactive Software Inc.	TTWO
TAL Education Group	XRS
TAL International Group Inc.	TAL
Talbots Inc.	TLB
Talecris Biotherapeutics Holdings Corp.	TLCR
Taleo Corp.	TLEO
Talisman Energy Inc.	TLM
TAM S.A.	TAM
TAN Range Exploration Corp.	TRE
Tanger Factory Outlet Centers Inc.	SKT
Targa Resources Corp.	TRGP

Targa Resources Partners LP	NGLS
Targacept Inc.	TRGT
Target Corp.	TGT
Tata Communications Ltd.	TCL
Tata Motors Ltd.	TTM
Taubman Centers Inc.	TCO
TC Pipelines LP	TCLP
TCF Financial Corp.	TCB
Team Inc.	TISI
Tech Data Corp.	TECD
Techne Corp.	TECH
Technology Sector SPDR	XLK
Teck Cominco Ltd.	TCK
TECO Energy Inc.	TE
Teekay LNG Partners LP	TGP
Teekay Offshore Partners LP	TOO
Teekay Shipping Corp.	TK
Teekay Tankers Ltd.	TNK
Tekelec Inc.	TKLC
Tele Norte Leste Participacoes SA	TNE
Telecom Argentina SA ADR	TEO
Telecom Corp. of New Zealand Ltd.	NZT
Telecom HOLDRs Trust	TTH
Telecom Italia S.p.A.	TI
Telecomunicacoes de Sao Paulo SA	TSP
Teledyne Tech. Inc.	TDY
Teleflex Inc.	TFX
Telefonica de Espana S.A. ADR	TEF
Telefonos De Mexico SA	TMX
Telephone & Data Systems Inc.	TDS

Telestone Technologies Corp.	TSTC
TeleTech Hldgs. Inc.	TTEC
TELUS Corp.	TU
Telvent Git SA	TLVT
Temple-Inland Inc.	TIN
Tempur Pedic Intl. Inc.	TPX
Tenaris SA	TS
Tenet Healthcare Corp.	THC
Tennant Co.	TNC
Tenneco Automotive Inc.	TEN
Tera Tech Inc	TTEK
Teradata Corp.	TDC
Teradyne Inc.	TER
Terex Corp.	TEX
Ternium S.A.	TX
Terra Nova Royalty Corp.	TTT
Tesco Corp.	TESO
Tesla Motors Inc.	TSLA
Tesoro Petroleum Corp.	TSO
Tessera Techs.	TSRA
TETRA Techs. Inc.	TTI
Teucrium Corn Futures	CORN
Teucrium WTI Crude Oil Fund	CRUD
Teva Pharma. Indus. Ltd.	TEVA
Texas Industries Inc.	TXI
Texas Instruments Inc.	TXN
Texas Roadhouse Inc.	TXRH
Textainer Group Holdings Limited	TGH
Textron Inc.	TXT
TFS Financial Corp.	TFSL

The Medicines Co.	MDCO
The Toro Co.	TTC
The9 Ltd.	NCTY
Theravance Inc.	THRX
Thermo Fisher Scientific INC.	TMO
Thomas & Betts Corp.	TNB
Thompson Creek Metals Company Inc.	TC
Thomson Reuters Corp.	TRI
Thomson/Reuters CRG Global Commodity Eq Fund	CRBQ
Thor Indus. Inc.	THO
Thoratec Labs Corp.	THOR
TIBCO Software Inc.	TIBX
TICC Capital Corp.	TICC
Tidewater Inc.	TDW
Tiffany & Co.	TIF
Tim Hortons Inc.	THI
TIM Participacoes SA	TSU
Timberland Co.	TBL
Time Warner Cable	TWC
Time Warner Inc.	TWX
Time Warner Telecom Inc.	TWTC
Timken Co.	TKR
Titan International Inc.	TWI
Titan Machinery Inc.	TITN
Titanium Metals Corp.	TIE
TiVo Inc.	TIVO
TJX Companies Inc.	TJX
TNS Inc.	TNS
Toll Brothers Inc.	TOL
Tollgrade Comms. Inc.	TLGD

Tootsie Roll Industries Inc.	TR
Torchmark Corp.	TMK
Toreador Resources Corp.	TRGL
Tornier NV	TRNX
Toronto Dominion Bank	TD
Total SA ADR	TOT
Total System Services Inc.	TSS
Tower Group Inc.	TWGP
Towers Watson & Co	TW
Toyota Motor Corp.	TM
TPC Group Inc	TPCG
Tractor Supply Co.	TSCO
Trade Station Group Inc.	TRAD
Transact Techns. Inc.	TACT
Transatlantic Holdings Inc.	TRH
TransCanada Corp.	TRP
TransDigm Group Inc.	TDG
TransGlobe Energy Corp.	TGA
Transmontaigne Partners LP	TLP
TravelCenters of America LLC	TA
Travelers Companies Inc. (The)	TRV
Tredegar Corp.	TG
Tree.Com Inc.	TREE
TreeHouse Foods Inc.	THS
Trex Co. Inc.	TREX
Triangle Petroleum Corp.	TPLM
TriMas Corp.	TRS
Trimble Navigation Ltd.	TRMB
Trina Solar Ltd.	TSL
Trinity Industries Inc.	TRN

Triple-S Management Corp.	GTS
Triquint Semiconductor Inc.	TQNT
Triumph Group Inc.	TGI
True Religion Apparel Inc.	TRLG
TrueBlue Inc.	TBI
TrustCo Bank Corp. NY	TRST
Trustmark Corp.	TRMK
TRW Automotive Hlds. Corp.	TRW
Tsakos Energy Navigation Ltd. ASA	TNP
TTM Technologies Inc.	TTMI
Tupperware Corp.	TUP
Turkcell Iletisim Hizmetleri AS	TKC
Tutor Perini Corp.	TPC
Two Harbors Investment Corp.	TWO
Tyco Electronics Ltd.	TEL
Tyco International Ltd.	TYC
Tyler Techs. Inc.	TYL
Tyson Foods Inc. Class A	TSN
U.S. Bancorp	USB
U.S. Global Investors Inc.	GROW
U.S. Steel Group	X
UBS AG	UBS
UBS E-TRACS Long Platinum Total Return ETN	PTM
UGI Corp.	UGI
UIL Holdings Corp.	UIL
Ulta Salon Cosmetics & Fragrance Inc.	ULTA
Ultimate Software Group Inc.	ULTI
Ultra Clean Holdings Inc.	UCTT
Ultra Petroleum Corp.	UPL
Ultrapar Holdings Inc.	UGP

Ultratech Inc.	UTEK
UMB Financial Corp.	UMBF
Umpqua Holdings Corp.	UMPQ
Under Armour Inc.	UA
UniFirst Corp.	UNF
Unilever NV	UN
Unilever PLC	UL
Unilife Corp.	UNIS
Union Drilling Inc.	UDRL
Union Pacific Corp.	UNP
Unisource Energy Corp.	UNS
Unisys Corp.	UIS
Unit Corp.	UNT
United America Indemnity Ltd.	GBLI
United Bankshares Inc.	UBSI
United Continental Holdings	UAL
United Dominion Realty Trust Inc.	UDR
United Financial Bancorp	UBNK
United Fire & Casualty Co.	UFCS
United Natural Foods Inc.	UNFI
United Online Inc.	UNTD
United Parcel Service Inc.	UPS
United Rentals Inc.	URI
United States 12 Month Natural Gas Fund LP	UNL
United States 12 Month Oil Fund LP	USL
United States Cellular Corp.	USM
United States Gasoline Fund	UGA
United States Natural Gas	UNG
United States Oil	USO
United States Short Oil Fund	DNO

United Stationers Inc.	USTR
United Techs. Corp.	UTX
United Therapeutics Corp.	UTHR
UnitedHealth Group Inc.	UNH
Unitrin Inc.	UTR
Universal American Corp.	UAM
Universal Corp.	UVV
Universal Display Corp.	PANL
Universal Electronics Inc.	UEIC
Universal Forest Products Inc.	UFPI
Universal Health Class B	UHS
Universal Insurance Holdings Inc.	UVE
Universal Tech. Institute Inc.	UTI
UnumProvident Corp.	UNM
Urban Outfitters Inc.	URBN
Uroplasty Inc.	UPI
URS Corp.	URS
US Airways Group Inc.	LCC
US Energy Corp.	USEG
US Gold Corp.	UXG
USA Mobility Inc.	USMO
USANA Health Sciences Inc.	USNA
USG Corp.	USG
U-Store-It Trust	YSI
USX - Marathon Group	MRO
UTI Worldwide Inc.	UTIW
Utilities HOLDRs Trust	UTH
Utilities Sector SPDR	XLU
V.F. Corp.	VFC
Vaalco Energy Inc.	EGY

Vail Resorts Inc.	MTN
Valassis Comms. Inc.	VCI
VALE SA	VALE.P
Valeant Pharmas. Intl.	VRX
Valero Energy Corp. (New)	VLO
Validus Holdings Ltd.	VR
Valley National Bancorp.	VLY
Valmont Indus. Inc.	VMI
Valspar Corp.	VAL
Value Click Inc.	VCLK
ValueVision Media Inc.	VVTV
VanceInfo Technologies Inc.	VIT
Vanda Pharma. Inc.	VNDA
Vanguard Dividend Appreciation	VIG
Vanguard Emerging Markets Stock	VWO
Vanguard Energy VIPERs	VDE
Vanguard Europe Pacific	VEA
Vanguard European Stock VIPERs	VGK
Vanguard Financials VIPERs	VFH
Vanguard FTSE All-World ex-US	VEU
Vanguard Growth VIPERs	VUG
Vanguard Health Care VIPERs	VHT
Vanguard High Dividend Yield	VYM
Vanguard Industrials VIPERs	VIS
Vanguard Info. Techn. VIPERs	VGT
Vanguard Intermediate-Term Bond	BIV
Vanguard Large Cap VIPERs	VV
Vanguard MCSI US Mid-Cap Growth	VOT
Vanguard Mega Cap 300	MGC
Vanguard Mega Cap 300 Growth	MGK

Vanguard Mega Cap 300 Value	MGV
Vanguard Mid Cap VIPERs	VO
Vanguard MSCI Investable Market Material	VAW
Vanguard MSCI US Mid Cap Value	VOE
Vanguard MSCI US Small Cap Growth	VBK
Vanguard MSCI US Small Cap Value	VBR
Vanguard Natural Resources LLC	VNR
Vanguard Pacific Stock VIPERs	VPL
Vanguard REIT VIPERs	VNQ
Vanguard S&P 500	VOO
Vanguard Small Cap. VIPERs	VB
Vanguard Total Bond Market	BND
Vanguard Total Stock Market VIPERs	VTI
Vanguard Value VIPERs	VTV
Varian Medical Systems	VAR
Varian Semi. Equip. Assoc. Inc.	VSEA
VASCO Data Security Intl. Inc.	VDSI
Vascular Solutions Inc.	VASC
VCA Antech Inc.	WOOF
Vector Group Ltd.	VGR
Vectren Corp.	VVC
Veeco Instruments Inc.	VECO
VelocityShares Long VIX Short Term ETN	VIIX
Venoco Inc.	VQ
Ventas Inc.	VTR
Veolia Environnement SA	VE
Vera Bradley Inc.	VRA
VeriFone Holdings Inc.	PAY
Verigy Ltd.	VRGY
Verint Systems Inc.	VRNT

Verisign Inc.	VRSN
Verisk Analytics Inc.	VRSK
Verizon Wireless	VZ
Vertex Pharma. Inc.	VRTX
Viacom Class A	VIA
Viacom Inc. Class B	VIA.B
Viad Corp.	VVI
ViaSat Inc.	VSAT
Vicor Corp.	VICR
Viewpoint Financial Group	VPFG
Vimpel-Communications	VIP
Virgin Media Inc.	VMED
VirnetX Holding Corp	VHC
ViroPharma Inc.	VPHM
Visa Inc.	V
Vishay Intertech. Inc.	VSH
Vishay Precision Group Inc.	VPG
VistaPrint Ltd.	VPRT
Visteon Corp.	VC
Vital Images Inc.	VTAL
Vitamin Shoppe Inc.	VSI
Vitesse Semiconductor Corp.	VTSS
Vivo Participacoes S.A.	VIV
VIVUS Inc.	VVUS
VMware Inc.	VMW
VocalTec Communications Ltd.	CALL
Vocus Inc.	VOCS
Vodafone AirTouch PLC	VOD
Volcano Corp.	VOLC
Volcom Inc.	VLCM

Volt Information Sciences Inc.	VISI
Volterra Semiconductor Corp.	VLTR
Vornado Realty Trust	VNO
Vulcan Materials	VMC
W&T Offshore Inc.	WTI
W.R. Berkley Corp.	WRB
W.R. Grace & Co.	GRA
Wabash National Corp.	WNC
Wabco Holdings Inc.	WBC
Waddell & Reed Fin.	WDR
Walgreen Co.	WAG
Wal-Mart Stores Inc.	WMT
Walter Energy Inc.	WLT
Warnaco Group Inc.	WRC
Warner Chilcott Ltd.	WCRX
Warner Music Group Inc.	WMG
Washington Federal Inc.	WFSL
Washington REIT	WRE
Waste Connections Inc.	WCN
Waste Management Inc.	WM
Waters Corp.	WAT
Watsco Inc	WSO
Watson Pharma. Inc.	WPI
Watts Water Techs. Inc.	WTS
Wausau Paper Corp.	WPP
Weatherford Intl. Inc.	WFT
Web.com Group Inc.	WWWW
WebMD Health Corp.	WBMD
Websense Inc.	WBSN
Webster Financial Corp.	WBS

Weight Watchers Intl. Inc.	WTW
Weingarten Realty Investors	WRI
Wellcare Health Plans Inc.	WCG
Wellpoint Health Networks Inc.	WLP
Wells Fargo & Co.	WFC
Werner Enterprises Inc.	WERN
WesBanco Inc.	WSBC
Wesco Intl. Inc.	WCC
West Pharma. Srvs. Inc.	WST
Westamerica Bancorp	WABC
Westar Energy Inc.	WR
Western Alliance Bancorp.	WAL
Western Digital Corp.	WDC
Western Gas Partners LP	WES
Western Refining Inc.	WNR
Western Union Co. (The)	WU
Westinghouse Air Brake Techs. Corp.	WAB
Westlake Chemical Corp.	WLK
Westport Innovations Inc.	WPRT
Weyerhaeuser Co.	WY
WGL Holdings Inc.	WGL
Whirlpool Corp.	WHR
Whiting Petroleum Corp.	WLL
Whiting USA Trust REIT	WHX
Whitney Holding Corp.	WTNY
Whole Foods Market Inc.	WFMI
Willbros Group Inc.	WG
Williams Companies Inc.	WMB
Williams Partners LP	WPZ
Williams-Sonoma Inc.	WSM

Willis Group Hldgs.	WSH
Wilson Greatbatch Tech. Inc.	GB
Wimm-Bill-Dann Foods OJSC	WBD
Windstream Corp.	WIN
Winn-Dixie Stores Inc.	WINN
Winnebago Industries Inc.	WGO
Wintrust Financial Corp.	WTFC
Wipro Ltd.	WIT
Wisconsin Energy	WEC
WisdomTree Dreyfus Brazilian Real	BZF
WisdomTree Dreyfus Chinese Yuan	CYB
WisdomTree Dreyfus Emerging Currency	CEW
WisdomTree Dreyfus Euro	EU
WisdomTree Dreyfus Indian Rupee	ICN
WisdomTree Dreyfus New Zealand Dollar	BNZ
WisdomTree Dreyfus South African Rand	SZR
WisdomTree India Earnings	EPI
WisdomTree Japan Hedged Equity	DXJ
WisdomTree Japan SmallCap Dividend	DFJ
WMS Industries Inc.	WMS
Wolverine World Wide Inc.	WWW
Wonder Auto Technology Inc.	WATG
Woodward Inc.	WWD
World Acceptance Corp.	WRLD
World Fuel Services Corp.	INT
World Wrestling Entertainment Inc.	WWE
Worthington Ind. Inc.	WOR
WPP Group PLC	WPPGY
Wright Express Corp.	WXS
Wright Medical Technology	WMGI

WuXi PharmaTech (Cayman) Inc.	WX
Wyndham Worldwide Corp.	WYN
Wynn Resorts Ltd.	WYNN
Xcel Energy Inc.	XEL
XenoPort Inc.	XNPT
Xerox Corp.	XRX
XETA Technologies Inc.	XETA
Xilinix Inc.	XLNX
XL Capital Ltd.	XL
Xueda Education Group American	XUE
Xyratex Ltd.	XRTX
Yahoo Inc.	YHOO
Yamana Gold Inc.	AUY
Yanzhou Coal Mining Co. Ltd.	YZC
Yingli Green Energy Holding Co. Ltd.	YGE
Yongye Intl. Inc.	YONG
Youku.com Inc. ADR	YOKU
YPF S.A.	YPF
Yuhe International Inc.	YUII
Yum Brands Inc.	YUM
ZAGG Inc.	ZAGG
Zebra Techs. Inc.	ZBRA
Zep Inc.	ZEP
Zhongpin Inc.	HOGS
Zimmer Hldgs. Inc.	ZMH
Zions Bancorp.	ZION
ZIOPHARM Oncology Inc.	ZIOP
Zipcar Inc.	ZIP
ZOLL Medical Corp.	ZOLL
Zoltek Companies Inc.	ZOLT

Zoran Corp.	ZRAN
Zumiez Inc.	ZUMZ
Zygo Corp.	ZIGO

ETFs (EXCHANGE TRADED FUNDS)

ETF Name	**Symbol**
SPDR TR UNIT SER 1	SPY
POWERSHARES QQQ TRUST UNIT SER 1	QQQQ
ISHARES TR RUSSELL 2000	IWM
SELECT SECTOR SPDR TR SBI INT-FINL	XLF
SELECT SECTOR SPDR TR SBI INT-ENERGY	XLE
ISHARES INC MSCI JAPAN	EWJ
ISHARES INC MSCI MALAYSIA	EWM
SEMICONDUCTOR HLDRS TR DEP RCPT	SMH
OIL SVC HOLDRS TR DEPOSTRY RCPT	OIH
ISHARES INC MSCI SINGAPORE	EWS
ISHARES INC MSCI BRAZIL	EWZ
DIAMONDS TR UNIT SER 1	DIA
ISHARES TR FTSE XNHUA IDX	FXI
ISHARES TR MSCI EAFE IDX	EFA
ISHARES INC MSCI AUSTRALIA	EWA
ISHARES TR DJ US REAL EST	IYR
POWERSHARES ETF TRUST AERSPC DEF PTF	PPA
ISHARES INC MSCI GERMAN	EWG
ISHARES INC MSCI HONG KONG	EWH
ISHARES TR MSCI EMERG MKT	EEM
ISHARES TR RUSL 2000 VALU	IWN
SELECT SECTOR SPDR TR SBI INT-UTILS	XLU

ISHARES TR RUSL 2000 GROW	IWO
STREETTRACKS SER TR SPDR S&P RTL	XRT
SELECT SECTOR SPDR TR SBI INT-INDS	XLI
MIDCAP SPDR TR UNIT SER 1	MDY
RETAIL HOLDRS TR DEP RCPT	RTH
ISHARES INC MSCI TAIWAN	EWT
ISHARES TR S&P GSTI SEMIC	IGW
VANGUARD INTL EQUITY INDEX FD EMR MKT ETF	VWO

ACTIVELY TRADED INDEXES

INDEX NAME	SYMBOL	EXPIRATION TYPE
NASDAQ 100 index	NDX	European style expiration
S&P 100 index	OEX	American style expiration
S&P 500 index	SPX	European style expiration
Dow Jones index	DJX	European style expiration
Russell 2000 index	RUT	European style expiration
S&P Midcap 400 Index	MID	European style expiration
Mini NDX Index	MNX	European style expiration
Mini S&P Index (1/10th of full size contract)	XSP	European style expiration
S&P 100 index	XEO	European style expiration

GLOSSARY

In order not to make this a long glossary list I've only included terms and phrases that are used in this book.

American-style Option - An option contract that may be exercised at any time before expiration date. Stock options and most exchange-traded-funds (ETF) have American Style expirations.

Assignment – The notice given to an option seller or writer informing him that the option he sold is being exercised by the option holder. It obligates the option seller to buy and take deliver of the underlying security from the option holder.

At-the-money - An option whose strike price is at parity to the current market price of the underlying security.

Call - An option that gives the holder the right, but not the obligation, to buy an underlying security at a contracted price for a specified period of time.

Closing purchase (options) – The purchase of an option by the original seller in order to reduce or eliminate a potential negative situation that could arise from a short position.

Closing sale (options) – The sale of an option to reduce or terminate a long position.

Covered call option sale – A trading strategy whereby one sells call options against an underlying security that he owns. It is called covered because the options sold are secured by the security that he owns.

Derivative security – Any financial instrument whose value is derived from the value of another underlying security.

Equity options - Options on shares of stock.

European-style option - An option contract that may be exercised only at the expiration date of the contract period.

As differentiated from American type options, European style cannot be exercised no matter how deep-in-the money the option value may be. (see below for definition of In-The-Money)

Exercise – An option is said to be exercised when the option holder invokes his right to buy the underlying security (in the case of calls) or sell the underlying security (in the case of puts). The seller of the option is then obligated to sell (in the case of calls) or buy (in the case of puts) the underlying security which may be stocks or index.

Exercise price – Also called the strike price, it is the price which the seller and buyer agree to if and when the option holder decides to exercise his option rights as stipulated in the option contract. It is the price that the underlying security will be valued at delivery.

Expiration date – The last date on which the option holder may exercise his right to buy or sell the underlying security of an option. After such date the right to exercise terminates.

In-the-money (ITM) – An ITM option is when a call option's strike price is less than the market price of the underlying security or, when a put option's strike price is greater than the market price of the underlying security.

Intrinsic value – The difference between the strike price and the amount by which an option is in-the-money (see above definition).

Long position – An option holder is said to have a long position when he is the option buyer as against being the option seller.

Margin maintenance requirement - The amount required by securities regulators to be deposited by option sellers in order to partially protect an uncovered or naked option position. The amount of margin deposit required may vary greatly depending on the chosen options broker.

Open interest: The number of outstanding options or futures contracts in the market. It is called 'open' because they are unliquidated meaning not closed contracts.

Option: The right, but not the obligation, to buy or sell an underlying instrument, such as a stock, a futures contract or an index value, at a specified price for a certain, fixed period of time.

Option Chain: A table or list of all the options that are available for a given underlying security, such as stock, index, commodity, futures, etc. It normally consists of two sections, a left side showing listings for call options and a right side showing listings for put options. In the center are the various strike prices available. On both the call and put sides are listed the last price at which a particular option was last traded, the current bid and ask quotes, and the open interest.

Option Holder: The purchaser of a call or put option.

Out-of-the-money (OTM) - An OTM option is when a call option's strike price is greater than the market price of the underlying security or, when a put option's strike price is less than the market price of the underlying security

Premium – Premium is just another term indicating the price of a call or put option as quoted in the markets.

Put - An option that gives the holder the right, but not the obligation, to sell an underlying security at a contracted price for a specified period of time.

Short position – The position taken by an option seller as opposed to that of an option holder who bought options and is said to be in a long position.

Straddle - An option position in which a call and a put with the same strike price and expiration are both bought (long straddle) or sold (short straddle).

Strangle - An option spread strategy involving a long put and a long call or a short put and a short call with different strikes but the same expiration. The most common strangles involve out-of-the-money options.

Strike price – Also called the exercise price, it is the price which the seller and buyer agree to if and when the option holder decides to exercise his option rights as stipulated in the option contract. It is the price that the underlying security will be valued at delivery.

Time value – That element of the option quote that is not dictated by real value but is determined purely on the amount of time left on the contract prior to maturity.

Uncovered call writing – An option position when one sells or writes a call option and he does not own the underlying security to cover the position in case of exercise.

Uncovered put writing - An option position when one sells or writes a put option and he does not have the corresponding short position in the underlying security or does not have the necessary cash equivalent to cover his potential liability in case of assignment.

Underlying security - The security that is the subject to being purchased or sold upon exercise or assignment of the option.

Volatility – Is what the market uses in measuring how stable or unstable an underlying security is taking into consideration the various factors that affect price behavior.

Writer – Another term for an option seller.

DISCLAIMER

The trading system discussed here, including examples using actual securities and price data, are strictly for illustrative and educational purposes only and should not be considered as complete, precise, or current. The writer is not a stockbroker and as such does not endorse, recommend or solicit to buy or sell securities. The written materials here are not a substitute for obtaining professional advice from a qualified person, firm or corporation. Consult the appropriate professional advisor for more complete and current information. Options involve risks and are not suitable for everyone. Prior to buying or selling options, an investor must receive a copy of "Characteristics and Risks of Standardized Options". Review this document at: http://www.cboe.com/Resources/Intro.asp. Copies may be obtained from your broker, from The Options Clearing Corporation, 440 S. LaSalle Street, 24th Floor, Chicago, IL 60605, or by calling 1-888-OPTIONS.

www.ingramcontent.com/pod-product-compliance
Lightning Source LLC
Chambersburg PA
CBHW061150220326
41599CB00025B/4425

9781607963691